HOLINESS IN THE CHURCH

Holiness in the Church

by Rev. John A. Hardon, S.J.

St. Paul Editions

IMPRIMI POTEST:
  Eamon G. Taylor, S.J.
  Provincial of the New York Province
February 24, 1976

IMPRIMATUR:
  ✠ Humberto Cardinal Medeiros
    Archbishop of Boston
April 26, 1976

PHOTO CREDITS:
  Brooks 26
  Dolan 156
  Terra   14, 50, 65, 120, 145

Library of Congress Cataloging in Publication Data.

    1. Spiritual life—Catholic authors—Addresses, essays,
lectures. 2. Holiness—Addresses, essays, lectures. 3. Monastic and religious life—Addresses, essays, lectures. I.
Title.
BX2350.2.H354   248'.48'2   76-15371

Printed in U.S.A. by the Daughters of St. Paul
50 St. Paul's Ave., Boston, Ma. 02130

The Daughters of St. Paul are an international
religious congregation serving the Church with
the communications media.

CONTENTS

Introduction 11

Part One
The Universal Call to Holiness

Our Call to Holiness 15
The Age of Martyrs Today 27
Christ and the World 41
Christ Our Way 51
Christ Our Light 63
Christ Our Strength............................... 73
Peace of Heart 81
Spiritual Joy 93

Part Two
Holiness in the Religious Life

Why the Religious Life? The Sanctification
   of the Church of Christ 103
The Essentials of Religious Life 121
Liberty – Choice, Love and Sacrifice......... 135
Religious Vocation – of Divine Origin 143
What Is a Religious Community Today?... 157
The Spiritual Personality of Religious
   Communities 171

Introduction

The purpose of this small volume of reflections on the spiritual life is to encourage those who read it to become more holy. What it has to say is not new, no more than Christ or Christianity is new. Yet there are times, like our own, when the truths we have always believed take on a very new meaning because they are seen to meet a deeply felt need in the Church in our day. The call to holiness is one of these truths that, until recently, we may have taken for granted as we casually pronounced the Creed that we believe in the one, holy, Catholic and apostolic Church.

But all that is changed now as we look upon a world torn by strife and conflict, and whole nations suffering under the oppressive hands of organized tyranny that has given the Church thousands of martyrs and confessors. In many sectors of the Church are problems so grave that nothing but the almighty hand of God can resolve them.

That is why a book on holiness in the Church is more than timely. It is critically necessary if we are ever to cope with the trials that confront the believing Christian in every walk of life and on every level of society. After all, what else is holiness than accepting the trials that God sends us and loving Him all the more because He gives us the opportunity to prove our loyalty to His providential will.

The fourteen essays that form the volume were originally given as conferences to priests, religious and the laity. They are being published under the auspices of the Institute on Religious Life in the hope that the message they contain may be of some service to the faithful in every state of life to draw closer to the infinite source of sanctity, which is Jesus Christ.

Part 1

THE
UNIVERSAL
CALL
TO
HOLINESS

Our Call
to Holiness

It is not often we hear about the duty of a Christian to become holy, except in a conference for religious or priests. And even then the subject may be offered apologetically, as though there was something poetic, or not quite real, in striving after sanctity.

One of the glories of the Second Vatican Council was its outspoken insistence not only that holiness is a realistic goal to strive for, but this is our special vocation as Christians. "All of Christ's faithful," we are told, "no matter what their rank or station, have a vocation to the fullness of the Christian life and the perfection of charity." In a word, we have all been called to become saints.

This broad statement of fact needs to be carefully examined for many reasons, not the least of which is that the Church today needs so many things. But she needs nothing more than sanctity among her faithful.

WHAT IS HOLINESS?

As with other facets of our faith, so here the meaning of sanctity is shrouded in mystery. In fact, it is a mystery. Yet it should not be an unintelligible mystery.

In one sense, everyone who is baptized and is in the state of grace is holy. And there are many passages, especially in St. Paul, that testify to this meaning of the term. But properly speaking, holiness is not only being in God's friendship; it is being Christlike.

What do we mean when we say that we are as holy as we are like Christ? We mean that Jesus Christ is the pattern for us to follow. The more we become like Him, the more holy we are. This stands to reason since Christ is God, and of course a person is only as holy as he is similar to God.

What we are saying is not as obvious as may at first sight appear. No doubt expressions like "the imitation of Christ," or "the following of Christ," or "walking in the footsteps of Christ" are familiar enough. But what do they say? They affirm the astounding fact that when God became man in the person of Jesus of Nazareth, that man was literally God walking on our earth, eating our food, breathing our air, and living in every way, except sin, the human life that we live. He did so not only to redeem us from Satan and hell, but to show us how we can with His grace become like Him in virtue.

When we are born into the world we already have the same nature that Christ had, and this through no effort or striving on our part. But we do not have the same holiness that He had, nor shall we ever achieve it. Nevertheless, we can and we should become ever more like Him, who is God, since this is the main reason He became like us, who are creatures and not God.

This is the key to a correct understanding of that strange invitation of the Savior to the rich young man, "If you will be perfect." It is also the key to His injunction that we should be perfect, as our heavenly Father is perfect.

The key is to know what Jesus meant by the word *perfect*. He could only have meant that since He is one with the Father, and God is perfectly holy, the closer we approximate His goodness the more·perfect we shall become. It is like producing a masterpiece of art, which is only as perfect as it perfectly imitates nature, or like a good reproduction if it closely duplicates the original.

That is what striving after perfection is all about. After the learned books on the subject have been read, it means trying with the help of His grace to become more and more like the man, Jesus, who was perfect in every human virtue because, though man, He was also God.

Time and again He bade us become like Him, "Learn of me, for I am meek and humble of heart.... If I, the Lord and Master, have washed your feet, you should wash each other's feet. I have given you an example so that you may copy what I have done to you.... I give you a new commandment: Love one another just as I have loved you." This is the formula of sanctity: Study the conduct of Christ and strive to do the same. If you do, and insofar as you do, you will become holy.

WE ARE ALL TO BE HOLY

As we read the Scriptures, it seems clear that all the faithful are called to become holy. There appear to be no exceptions. Words like *blameless* and *spotless* and *wholly pleasing to God* are thematic in the writings of St. Paul and the other apostles. Moreover, as we look at the history of the apostolic Church, we see that the faithful were indeed faithful. A single episode like that of Ananias and Sapphira, who were punished by sudden death for withholding some of their property from the common fund, illustrates how totally dedicated the first Christians were expected to be. And they were. Those who were not were ostracized from the community of believers and their conversion earnestly prayed for.

As time went on, however, with increased numbers there was also increased mediocrity. True enough, the Church still had multitudes of highly committed members, and she could always honestly call herself holy, not only in offering the means of sanctification but in producing saints. Yet the number of quite ordinary Christians with no great zeal for holiness, and even quite sinful Christians in the fold, has been the Church's record over the centuries.

We are here dealing with one of the imponderables of Christianity and only God knows the full explanation of what we shall try to explain. But ever since the apostolic age there has been a remarkable correlation between urgency of the Church's needs in a given period and the quality of many of her people. It seems that Providence provides for these needs by raising up men and women in all walks of life who become beacons of light to the rest of the Church and a leaven in the mass of the Christian faithful.

In fact, we can go further to say that the whole moral tone of the Church in such critical times is supernaturally elevated to cope, as it were, with the crisis that the Mystical Body is faced with. Times of trial and defection thus become times of growth and perfection. When sin abounds then sanctity will ever more abound according to some hidden law of rehabilitation that God invariably provides for the Body of Christ which is His Church.

Viewed in this light, the reminder of the Second Vatican Council that we are all called to holiness takes on profound meaning. No doubt this universal vocation to sanctity is always valid. But there are times when it is not only valid; it is necessary.

Let us go into this a little more deeply: to see how, or better why, more than ever today the Church wants because she needs to have all who are still faithful to her teaching to also be more than ordinary Christians. They must be; no matter how jarring or strange the word may sound, they must be holy.

Why so? Because in today's world of doctrinal confusion and moral turmoil, it requires more than ordinary virtue even to survive.

Take the single social pressure on today's family. Husband and wife are expected, as Catholics, to remain faithful to one another until death. Yet everywhere in the United States the culture in which they live favors easy and frequent divorce; plural and companion marriages, or cohabitation without marriage; or swapping of marriage partners.

The same can be said about priests and religious, whose image in our country has been distorted in the extreme. They are still expected to remain celibate when celibacy has become, in the popular mind, almost a symbol of oddity or lack of maturity or even a screen that hides a life of moral misconduct.

Certainly no ordinary dedication to the priesthood or a life of the evangelical counsels can survive the studied onslaught of those who control the mind-forming media of our society.

UNITY BUT NOT UNIFORMITY

There is, therefore, need for extraordinary virtue to keep alive the practice of Christian virtue in secularized cultures in Euro-America. The need is not only for personal endurance to withstand the subtle and overt pressures to conformity that oppress the conscientious Catholics like a fetid atmosphere. The need is also because a society cannot reform itself without reformers, whose reformation is mainly effected by their constancy in the face of trial, and who influence their fellowmen to conversion mainly by the graces they merit before God through their heroic attachment to the will of God.

But there is one more feature of holiness in our day that deserves careful scrutiny. It is the question of what kind of holiness this means.

The question is highly practical because many people, especially the laity, are wondering where all of this leads. Most of the books on the spiritual life which they read are evidently written for persons in the priesthood or the cloister. So they are confused because it seems, they feel, that to grow in holiness one must separate himself and live apart from the noise and crowd of the world.

At the same time, priests and religious are confused because theories are accumulating which say that the asceticism of former days was either all wrong, or it is out-of-date today. The asceticism of the ancients, say up to the Second Vatican Council, stressed interiority, recollection of heart, mastery of one's passions, humility and docility of spirit, and much prayer in the form of meditations and pious aspirations throughout the day. But nowadays, the faithful are told, all of these former things have passed away.

The issues that this shift in spirituality implies are too broad and wide-ranging to do any more than advert to them here. What should be made clear, however, is that in spite of all the fanfare there has not been any reversal in the pursuit of holiness in our day. All the essentials of the sanctifying process that were valid in the days of St. Paul, or Augustine, or Aquinas, or Margaret Mary, or Theresa of Lisieux are still valid today.

Let us be clear about fundamentals. No one is saying that the pursuit of holiness by a workman in the factory is identical with that of a priest in the rectory; nor that growth in Christian perfection is to be sought in exactly the same way by a salesgirl and a cloistered nun. And one of the errors, not to say tragedies, of our day is the idea that it makes no difference. It does, and the sooner some people learn the facts of life in this matter, the better for the Church, and within the Church, for all levels of the faithful.

While saying this, however, we dare not conclude that because there are different states of life, in all of which a person can become holy, therefore each state of life is a closed system; therefore the basic means of becoming more Christlike are radically different.

Not at all. In spite of their bewildering variety and the great differences that obtain, say, between the responsibilities of marriage and the duties of religious life, all who strive after holiness must use certain means offered them by the Church. Otherwise what began as a strong desire will end up in disillusionment and failure.

It is not our business at this point to go into great detail. Yet we cannot omit mentioning some of these indispensable means of holiness which, in greater or less measure, are available to every sincere Catholic if he but takes the time and effort to discover them. Let me just mention four of them, with only a brief word of explanation, namely, state of life, the Eucharist, personal prayer, and regular self-evaluation.

Each person now finds himself in a particular state of life. Faith assures us this is not the result of chance. It is part, and I would say the indispensable part of God's providence in our regard. We are Christians who do not believe in reincarnation. We believe we have only one life in this world, and after death comes judgment and the decision on our particular final destiny. It is God's will, then, that we work out our salvation *and* our sanctification within the framework of the state of life to which we should quietly believe we have been called. It is in this context, and no other, that God wants us to serve Him not just faithfully but very faithfully. If we do, we shall become holy. If we search elsewhere, or try to straddle the states of life, we shall hopefully save our souls but we shall not achieve sanctity.

The Eucharist is for all of us, and not only for priests and nuns. In fact, unless priests and religious are devoted to the Eucharist, as Mass, Holy Communion and Real Presence, they will lose their hold on virtue and, as happens to so many today, even lose their Catholic faith. It is Christ in the Eucharist who should be the unqualified center of our spiritual life, from whom and through whom we become more like Him. So that apart from the Eucharist, sanctity may be aspired to but it will never be achieved.

Personal prayer, by which I mean easy conversation with God during the day, is as necessary for holiness as the air we breathe is necessary to sustain life. This is not as difficult or exotic as may seem. The secret is to put our minds to it, literally. Once we decide that we shall regularly and frequently have God on our minds, we will share with Him those myriad thoughts that most people are prone to discuss only with themselves. Out of intimate conversation with God will grow intimate friendship with God, which is practically a definition of sanctity. The key is to really want to do so.

Finally, if we want to grow in virtue we must daily, at least once a day, stop to look at ourselves and take stock of ourselves. Call it examination of conscience, call it spiritual inventory, call it moral self-appraisal. Names do not matter. Nor is the length of time spent in this important interior reflection so important. What is important is that we are convinced this should be done and do it. How strange that every respectable business establishment, from the national corporation to the local grocery store, assumes the need for keeping records, making a daily account of, say, sales and amount of income. Yet some of us believe that the most important business in life, which is the pursuit of God's will and growth in the likeness of His Son, can succeed without planning or management and, by some miracle, can actually thrive on being haphazard and exposed to every whim of chance.

In the present stage of the Church's history, those will become holy who are no less but more serious about what they are doing than the children of this world who are ever so wise in their search for earthly success and the pursuit of worldly gain.

2. *Holiness in the Church*

The Age of Martyrs Today

It must seem odd to some people even to talk about a subject like, "The Age of Martyrs Today." Martyrs, we are inclined to think, are those ancient men and women in the first centuries of the Church whom we commemorate by name in the Canon of the Mass when we pray, "We honor the apostles and martyrs," and then name, after the apostles, "Linus, Cletus, Clement, Sixtus, Cornelius, Cyprian, Lawrence, Chrysogonus, John and Paul, Cosmas and Damian." Linus, the first mentioned of the twelve, died as Pope in the first centuries. Cosmas and Damian were twin brother physicians who shed their blood in the early fourth century.

Consequently, unless we take stock of ourselves, martyrs are not commonly associated with the later history of the Church, and certainly not with our own times. What a miscalculation!

A conservative estimate places the total number of martyrs who died for Christ up to the liberation edict of Constantine in 313 A.D. at around one hundred thousand. And we call that period the age of persecution or the age of martyrs. Yet, the number of Christians who have died for their faith since 1900 is several million. There have been more Christian martyrs since the turn of the present century than in all the preceding centuries put together.

It is no wonder, then, that the Second Vatican Council in its Constitution on the Church, in speaking of the universal call to holiness, went out of its way to identify martyrdom as one of the marks of holiness in our day. The passage deserves to be quoted in full:

"Since Jesus, the Son of God, manifested His charity by laying down His life for us, so too no one has greater love than he who lays down his life for Christ and His brothers. From the earliest times, then, some Christians have been called upon—and some will always be called upon—to give the supreme testimony of their love to all men, but ⌐specially to persecutors.

"The Church, then, considers martyrdom as an exceptional gift and as the fullest proof of love. By martyrdom a disciple is transformed into an image of his Master by freely accepting death for the salvation of the world—as well as his conformity to Christ in the shedding of his blood. Although few are presented such an opportunity, nevertheless all must be prepared to confess Christ before men. They must be prepared to make this profession of faith even in the midst of persecutions, which will never be lacking to the Church, in following the way of the cross."

Elsewhere in its declarations, the Council returned to the same theme: that the faithful should be ready and willing to suffer for Christ, by a bloody martyrdom if they receive this precious grace and certainly by a bloodless martyrdom in the footsteps of Jesus crucified.

There is so much here to meditate on and put into practice that I think we should first get our bearings. Two basic questions must be answered, namely, "What is martyrdom?" and "What are the forms of martyrdom recognized by the Church with which we can identify ourselves?" Otherwise the subject will be interesting perhaps but irrelevant. And martyrdom is not irrelevant today.

WHAT IS MARTYRDOM?

The best description of martyrdom was given by Christ Himself just before He ascended into heaven. "You will receive power when the Holy Spirit comes on you," He told the disciples, "and then you will be my witnesses not only in Jerusalem but throughout Judea and Samaria, and indeed to the ends of the earth" (Acts 1:8).

Here we have capsulized in one sentence the motive power of martyrdom, its nature, and its apostolic purpose.

The source of strength to suffer for Christ comes finally from the Holy Spirit, who is said to give power. In the language of the New Testament, this power is called *dunamis* (dynamism) and is the same kind of power by which miracles can be worked.

The nature of martyrdom is to witness, except that when Christ spoke to the disciples He did not say "You shall be my witnesses," but "You shall be my martyrs *(marturoi),*" which

tells us exactly what we want to know. The
essence of being a martyr is to be a witness. And
we know what a witness does. He gives testimony publicly that something he saw or heard
is true. He has experience of a fact or an event,
and as a witness he declares that what he says
(or signs his name to) is so. He gives evidence
to others that what he testifies to should be believed. Why? Because he personally knows.

We are liable to miss the preceding adjective
"my" in the clause "You shall be my martyrs."
This prefix is crucial. Those who are martyrs
are witnesses to Christ. They testify, if need be
with their blood, that what they believe is true
because they have known Christ. The implication is that in order to be a witness, even to martyrdom, one must have experienced Christ, in a
way comparable to what Peter told the early
Christians: "You did not see him, yet you love
him. And still without seeing him, you are already filled with a joy so glorious that it cannot
be described, because you believe" (1 Pt. 1:8).

So it was in the apostolic age, and so it is
in ours. In order to witness to Christ we must
believe in Him so strongly that we are filled with
His joy. This joy is, of course, as Peter explained,
not unalloyed with pain. But it is genuine and
unmistakable. It is also profoundly communica-
ble. In fact, one of the paradoxes of martyrdom
is the positive happiness that a strongly committed follower of Christ has in suffering for
Christ.

This is brought out dramatically by St. Luke
in describing the second summons of the apostles before the Sanhedrin, after they had been
warned not to preach about the Savior. The apostles were flogged and warned again not to speak

in the name of Jesus. As they left the jail where they had been scourged, they were "glad to have had the honor of suffering humiliation for the sake of the name" (Acts 5:40-41).

FORMS OF MARTYRDOM

There is more than passing value in seeing what are the different forms of martyrdom recognized in Christianity. The special value is to help us identify with one or another of these types, at the risk of having this mystery of our faith evaporate into academic theory. And martyrdom is no theory. It is a palpable fact of every true follower of Christ.

In making our reflections, we deliberately transmit what is not pertinent to our purpose: the veneration we have for martyrs who have already gone to their reward, whether they are officially recognized by the Church or not. And most martyrs have never been raised to the honors of the altar. There are simply too many of them!

Our concern is exclusively with the martyrdom that we can ourselves somehow *practice*, or *exercise*, or whatever verb is most appropriate for being "my martyrs" as Christ foretold that His staunch followers in every age were expected to be.

Martyrdom of Blood. The most obvious form of martyrdom and the paradigm for all the rest is that of blood. It means that a person is given the option, overt or at least implicit, of either betraying Christ or dying for Christ. He chooses death rather than betrayal and as a result merits a martyr's crown.

There is a mysterious reversal of roles here, between what happened when sin first entered the world and what happens every time a martyr lays down his life rather than become a traitor.

In the case of our first parents, death was incurred by sinning; in martyrdom sainthood is attained by dying. To the martyrs, their persecutors offer the alternative: either abjure the faith or die. And the martyrs choose to suffer for the faith when the first sinners had no choice but to suffer for their infidelity.

We see here the foundation for our belief. Christ, the great Martyr, expiated the sins of mankind by undergoing the death penalty which, except for man's sinfulness, would never have been imposed by God.

Although the Second Vatican Council reminds us that the grace of a martyr's death is a special gift not vouchsafed to many, in our day it has been conferred on thousands. This can teach us more than one lesson, but none more surely than the enormity of today's sins, seeing that so much dedicated blood has been shed by Christ's chosen ones to join with Christ in expiation and in an urgent plea for God's mercy.

Count up the crimes of infanticide in a country like the United States; the selfish cruelty of unfaithful husbands and wives leaving hundreds of thousands of children stranded from broken homes; the mounting crimes of violence; and whole nations plunged into war; the cold neglect of the rights of the Creator who is ignored and ridiculed and blasphemed even by His consecrated religious and priests.

There is a divine purpose in the martyrdom of blood. It is through blood that the world was first redeemed, and it is still through blood that the fruits of this redemption are applied to a sinning human race.

One thing we dare not forget is that these present-day martyrs are our fellow-members of the Mystical Body. Through their sufferings we are all made richer, as through their merits the whole Church becomes more holy.

Martyrdom of Persecution.

Not all the faithful who suffer for Christ also die for Christ. Opposition to the Christian faith and way of life does not always end in violent death for the persecuted victims.

Consequently, it is well to distinguish between what may be called martyrdom of blood and martyrdom of opposition which is bloodless indeed but no less—and sometimes more—painful to endure.

Immediately there comes to mind the persecution of the Church in Communist-occupied countries behind the iron or bamboo curtain. The persecution often ends in death, if not before the firing squad then after years of imprisonment in Siberia or some labor camp.

Not all the victims of persecution die at the hands of a godless government. Millions more are ostensibly free to walk the streets and live in a home. Yet they are, in effect, deprived of every human liberty to practice their religion and to serve Christ according to their faith. If they teach their children catechism, the parents are prevented from enjoying such privileges as decent living quarters or any kind of skilled job. If they are seen attending church, they are first warned, then threatened, and finally penalized—even to the loss of all their possessions.

So the sorry tale goes on, and has been going on for years in spite of the conspiracy of silence in our American press.

But that is not the whole picture. We need to shake ourselves into awareness that our country, too, is undergoing persecution. It is no less real for being more subtle, and no less painful for being perpetrated in the name of democracy.

What do I mean? I mean that any priest or religious, any married or single person in America who wishes to sincerely and fully live up to his religious commitment finds countless obstacles in his way and experiences innumerable difficulties that accumulatively can demand heroic fortitude to overcome and withstand.

All we have to do is place the eight beatitudes in one column and the eight corresponding attitudes of our culture in another column, and compare the two. Where Christ advocates poverty, the world despises the poor and canonizes the rich. Where Christ praises gentleness, the world belittles meekness and extols those who succeed by crushing anyone that stands in the way. Where Christ encourages mourning and sorrow for sin, the world revels in pleasure and the noise of empty laughter. Where Christ promises joy only to those who seek justice and holiness, the world offers satisfaction in the enjoyment of sin. Where Christ bids us forgive and show mercy to those who have offended us, the world seeks vengeance and its law courts are filled with demands for retribution. Where Christ blesses those who are pure of heart, the world scoffs at chastity and makes a god of sex. Where Christ tells the peaceful that they shall

be rewarded, the world teaches just the opposite in constant rebellion and violence and
massive preparation for war. And where Christ
teaches the incredible doctrine of accepting
persecution with patience and resignation to
God's will, the world dreads nothing more than
criticism and rejection; and human respect,
which means acceptance by society, is the
moral norm.

As anyone trying to live out
the beatitudes knows, the world not only does
not believe in them but, with legal and financial
and psychological power at its disposal, opposes
those who do not accept the secularism of our
day.

Why the opposition? It is finally hidden in
the mystery of evil but we get some inkling of
what lies behind the studied persecution by
the worldly of the virtuous in a little known
passage from the Book of Wisdom. The passage
was written in the first century before Christ.
It might as well have been written yesterday.

There are two parts to this biblical analysis
of why worldly people persecute those who are
trying to serve God.

In part one, the godless (as they are called)
say to themselves with misguided reasoning
that all they have to look for is what this world
offers them.

"Come, then," they argue with themselves,
"let us enjoy what good things there are, use
this creation with the zest of youth. Let none
of us forego his part in our orgy, let us leave the
signs of our revelry everywhere."

Next they turn their attention to the faithful believers who are a standing rebuke to the
godless. Here is what they say:

"As for the virtuous man who is poor, let us oppress him; let us not spare the widow, nor respect old age, white-haired with many years. Let our strength be the yardstick of virtue, since weakness argues its own futility. Let us lie in wait for the virtuous man, since he annoys us, and opposes our way of life, reproaches us for our breaches of the law and accuses us of playing false to our upbringing.

"Before us he stands, a reproof to our way of thinking; the very sight of him weighs our spirits down.

"Let us test him with cruelty and torture, and thus explore this gentleness of his, and put his endurance to the proof" (Wisdom 2:6-19).

This is the way they reason, the sacred author explains, but they are misled. Their malice blinds them. So it does. But in the meantime their malice also wreaks its hatred on all who try to serve God and refuse to compromise their religious convictions for the pottage of acceptance by the crowd.

Martyrdom of Witness. We still have one more type of martyrdom to reflect on, and it is, in a way, the most pervasive of all because no follower of Christ can escape it. This is the martyrdom of witness.

What do we mean by martyrdom of witness and how does it differ from the other two? It differs from them in that, even in the absence of active opposition—the imitation of Christ must always face passive opposition. From whom? From those who lack a clear vision of the Savior or who, having had it, lost their former commitment to Christ.

All that we have seen about the martyrdom by violence applies here too, but the method of opposition is different. Here the firm believer in the Church's teaching authority; the devoted servant of the papacy; the convinced pastor who insists on sound doctrine to his flock; the dedicated religious who want to remain faithful to their vows of authentic poverty, honest chastity, and sincere obedience; the firm parents who are concerned about the religious and moral training of their children and are willing to sacrifice generously to build and care for a Christian family — natural or adopted — such persons will not be spared also active criticism and open opposition. But they must especially be ready to live in an atmosphere of coldness to their deepest beliefs.

Sometimes they would almost wish the opposition were more overt and even persecution would be a welcome change. It is the studied indifference of people whom they know and love, of persons in their own natural or religious family, of men and women whose intelligence they respect and whose respect they cherish.

This kind of apathy can be demoralizing and, unless it finds relief, can be devastating.

To continue living a Christ-like life in this kind of environment is to practice the martyrdom of witness. Why witness? Because it means giving testimony to our deep religious convictions although all around us others are giving their own example to the contrary.

It means giving witness twice over: once on our own behalf as the outward expression of what we internally believe and once again on behalf of others whose conduct is not only different from ours but contradicts it.

Wherein lies the martyrdom? It lies in the deprivation of good example to us on the part of our contemporaries, and in the practice of Christian virtue in loneliness, because those who witness what we do are in the majority — numerically or psychologically — and we know they are being challenged and embarrassed by the testimony. We witness to them, indeed, but they are not pleased to witness who we are, what we stand for, what we say, or what we do.

Notwithstanding all of this, however, it behooves us to look at the positive side of the picture. We must remind ourselves that this witness of ours is not so sterile as we may suppose. Quite the contrary. Although we may be, or at least feel, often quite alone, we are not alone at all. Not infrequently our severest critics can become our strongest admirers. In any case, witness that we give by living up to the conviction of our faith is surely demanding on human nature. That is why we call it martyrdom. But it is a witness to the truth and God's grace is always active in the hearts of everyone whose path we cross.

If we would know the power of this martyrdom of witness we have only to read the annals of the early Church. The handful of believers whom Peter baptized on Pentecost Sunday were as a drop in the immense culture surrounding the Mediterranean Sea. Yet see what happened. This small group of convinced faithful were able, in less than three hundred years, to turn the tide of paganism in the Roman Empire. For long time they were deprived even of the basic civil rights accorded other citizens. They were often hunted like animals, and the catacombs tell us that they had to hide when celebrating the liturgy and hide the tombs of their revered dead.

But their patience and meekness finally prevailed. Yes, but only because it was supported by unbounded courage, born not of their own strength but of the power that Christ promised to give all His followers that shall witness to His name everywhere. This promise is just as true today. All that we need is to trust in the Spirit whom we possess, and never grow weary in giving testimony to the grace we received.

This is what Christ was talking about when He told us not to hide our virtues but to allow them to be publicly seen, like a candle on a candlestick or a city on a mountain top. We should not be afraid that by such evidence of our good works we shall become vain or proud. Of course this is always a temptation we must strive to overcome. But in the normal course of Providence we shall be protected from vainglory by the cost in humiliation that witnessing to a holy life inevitably brings. There will have to be enough death to self and enough ignoring of human respect to keep us from getting proud in our well-doing. God will see to that. On our part, we must be willing to pay the price of suffering in doing good, which is another name for being a living martyr, that is, a courageous witness to the life of Christ in the world today.

Christ
and
the World

There is so much talk these days about Christians relating to the world that some analysis of what this means seems imperative. Certainly we cannot hope to grow in the likeness of Christ unless we know something of the mind of Christ regarding the world.

Not the least difficulty we face, however, is to know not so much what Christ meant by the world, because He meant many things, but how He wants us to look at the world and deal with it on all the principal levels of our meeting the world.

At the risk of oversimplifying a complex subject, we can say that the New Testament recognizes two principal notions of the world. They are quite distinctive, even though in each case the biblical record speaks of them as "the world." Naturally our attitude toward each of these "worlds" will be different, no less than Christ's was different. I would not hesitate to say that failure at this very point, in not adequately distinguishing between world and world, is the source of much confusion and perhaps the main reason why so many well-intentioned people have been misled. They have mistaken one kind of world for another and, as a result, are spending their energies on the wrong object, which is another name for wasted effort.

THE WORLD AS GOD'S UNIVERSE

There is an obvious sense in which the world is the universe that God created. It is in this sense that St. John opens his Gospel by saying that "all things were made by him," that is, by the Word who is God. It is also in this sense that Christ, according to St. John, spoke of the glory which He had with the Father from eternity, before the creation of the world. It is finally in this sense that John in his Apocalypse tells us there will be a new heaven and a new earth, after the end of the present world, when God will reunite human souls with their bodies and produce a new world of beauty that will never end.

This is the present world of space and time. It is the world that has, as we say, developed in speed and opportunities for human satisfaction, in giving more people more food, more ease, more enjoyment, more life expectancy, more convenience, more comfort—and correspondingly less physical pain and less need for physical exertions than, until a century ago, was ever thought possible.

This is the world about which God speaks in Genesis when He said it was good. It *is* good because, on this level of our reflection, the world reflects what God intends it to be, and whatever corresponds to the will of God is certainly good.

Can we better describe what this means? Yes, the world of God's creation is all that He has made, insofar as *He* made it. So that what we are describing is the handiwork of God. It is the world of earth and sky, and all the grandeur and delicacy which this implies. It is the world of the sun, moon and stars above us, the mountains, seas and fertile fields around us, the beasts that walk the earth, the fishes in the waters and the birds of the air. It is the world of the atom and the cosmic ray. It is, in a word, the world that we can see, either with the eyes of our body or the more penetrating eyes of the mind.

Does this world include other human beings besides "myself"? Yes, indeed.

What is less obvious, however, is that the world of God's creation is not only, so to speak, what God has made, but what He is still making. It includes, therefore, the whole complex of God's enduring providence in the world in which we live. It emphatically includes all those myriad things we call "happenings" but that faith tells us are not happenings at all. They are so many manifestations of divine wisdom and goodness, no less than what might be called the existing universe. Both are creations, of course, but where the one is already made, the other is still in formation under the provident hand of God.

What should be our attitude toward this world? It should be an attitude of admiration and gratitude. It should also be an attitude of prudence, whereby we decide with God's grace how we ought to use what the Lord of the universe has so lovingly and lavishly bestowed on us, and so constantly places into our lives.

We are to use this world of size and shape and color and sound, of life and movement and feeling and joy insofar as it helps us reach the destiny for which we were made.

Is this easy to do? No, it is not. It requires careful forethought on our part to keep from being so enamored of God's creatures as to forget their Creator. It calls for shrewd selectivity in our choice of what we see and hear, what we taste and touch, where we go and how long we stay, and with whom we share our affections and in what way.

Nor can we object that everything that God made is good. So let us eat and drink and be merry, since every satisfaction in this world is made possible by God's providence and therefore is holy.

This kind of naiveté is very common. It is also sad, because even experience, not to say faith, tells us that not everything which is good is good for us. Either we train ourselves to self-mastery in the right use of creatures or we become their slave. Every person who allows himself to be deceived on the right use of creatures in time finds himself a victim of his passions—whether of gluttony or avarice or envy or lust or pride.

How then are we to use this wonderful world of people and things? We are to use it as a means to an end, not as an end (or goal) in itself. It is in this sense that St. Paul tells us to live in this world as travelers on the way to God. Naturally it takes faith to see this. But what are we believers for if not to know the difference between a temporary lodging and our real home?

THE WORLD AS SIN

Although using the same word, *world*, in the same sermon at the Last Supper, Christ meant two opposite things by the term. If He said He was not asking the Father to take His followers out of the world of creation, He also said He was praying that they might be delivered from the world of sin.

It is worth quoting in context what the Second Vatican Council says about this sober meaning of what some people never distinguish when they casually speak about adapting Christianity to the world.

"A monumental struggle against the powers of darkness pervades the whole history of man. The battle was joined from the very origins of the world and will continue until the last day, as the Lord has attested. Caught in this conflict, man is obliged to wrestle constantly if he is to cling to what is good, nor can he achieve his own integrity without great efforts and the help of God's grace.

"That is why Christ's Church, trusting in the design of the Creator, acknowledges that human progress can serve man's true happiness, yet she cannot help echoing the Apostle's warning, 'Be not conformed to this world' (Rom. 12:2). Here by the world is meant that spirit of pride and malice which transforms into an instrument of sin those human energies intended for the service of God and man" (Vatican Council II, *Constitution on the Church in the Modern World*, III, 37).

Needless to say, this world of malice and pride cannot be compromised with. It is worse than useless to talk about involvement in this world, or adjustment to its philosophy, or conforming to its signs of the times. It is tragedy. And the most tragic part of it is that those who advocate this kind of aggiornamento are unaware of their folly. They are so convinced that the future of Christianity lies in adaptation to this world that even to suggest they might be wrong is to expose oneself to recrimination and destruction or, if that is not possible, to ostracism.

As we might suppose, the world of "malice and pride" does not appear to be malicious or proud. It poses, in the words of St. Ignatius, as an angel of light or, in today's jargon, as an angel of liberation from tryanny. Its access to the media of communication has given it power to mold the human mind, to reshape the meaning of language, to change men's pattern of thinking to such depth and extent that some people are unable even to grasp the possibility of what is taking place. Even to talk this way, for not a few of our contemporaries — often learned and well-meaning — is to indulge in macabre fancy.

Yet it is this world that is opposed to Christ on principle. It does not believe that human progress in this world can serve man's true happiness. It holds that such progress *is* man's true happiness.

This world thrives on adaptation, but in reverse. It uses the developments of science not to help man but to destroy him spiritually. It uses the discoveries of human genius not to assist man in his moral life, to greater peace among men and greater love of God, but to incite conflict among men and to alienate them from God. It uses the marvels of social communication not to strengthen the bonds of faith in Christian community but to mobilize power in the hands of a few who then manipulate their fellowmen as puppets to do their master's bidding — while drugging their victims into insensibility by appealing to "co-responsibility," "shared responsibility," "new morality," "freedom from male tyranny," and the need for being "relevant to the modern age."

There are many implications that follow for the believing Catholic. Not the least of these is great prudence, not in the popular sense of mere caution but in the biblical sense of being, in Christ's language, as simple as doves and as wise as serpents.

Simplicity is not enough in dealing with this world about which Christ made that awful statement, "I pray not for the world." What He meant was that He does not, because He cannot, pray for the success of evil or the advancement of sin.

We hear a great deal nowadays, and rightly, about the need for reconciliation. But let us not be deceived. It would not be reconciliation to reconcile ourselves to the world which faith tells us is opposed on principle to Christ. It would be betrayal. And the betrayal is unfortunately all too easy because people are deceived by the appearance of evil under the guise of good.

Let us be specific. The exercise of ecclesiastical authority in the past had not infrequently been unfeeling, unkind and sometimes unjust. It was good to correct these abuses and make the Church's leaders more responsible to Christ's injunction that bishops in dioceses and superiors in religious communities be humble in their use of authority and not lord it over those whose faith alone sustains their obedience. But what happened? A new theory of speculative theology is now widely current which claims that no one, with stress on the "one"—no one in the Church's structure has the right to command obedience. Instead of bishops holding a divine right to govern in Christ's name, priests' organizations under a variety of beguiling names are the actual governing body and the bishop is only a spokesman for the priests. They decide, not he.

No doubt much of this inversion of Roman Catholic ecclesiology is still mostly in learned monographs published in America and Europe. No doubt, too, that reduction of this theory to practice is meeting resistance in most dioceses from the bishops, supported by the Pope. But the seeds of evasion of episcopal authority have been sown, and the harvest of bad fruit is already being reaped in more than one part of the Church of God.

In much the same way, situation ethics has intruded itself into the Catholic Church. Too often in the past, the objective principles of Christian morality were applied in a wooden and un-Christlike fashion. Norms of conduct prescribed by the Church were sometimes treated as though mercy and charity were not also, and primary, moral norms. There was a crying need for reform, and the Second Vatican Council made it clear that the much-needed reformation was on the way.

But again what happened? At first more covertly but by now openly, many formerly respected spokesmen for the Church's morality and canon law are telling the faithful that the whole corpus of moral legislation is not only outmoded but obsolete. Not a single precept of the Gospels is any longer preceptive, we are told, not even the sanctity of human life. The new norm of the new morality is the behavior pattern of civil society. Surely the Church does not want to be out of step with what is obviously a contraceptive, abortive, extra-maritally sexual, maritally unstable, and compulsively permissive American culture?

EPILOGUE

Against the background of the foregoing reflections, it may seem pointless to still talk about holiness or growth in Christian perfection. But it is not pointless; it is the highest wisdom to encourage ourselves to above-average practice of virtue. Why so? Because holiness clarifies the mind, as the beatitude tells us: "How happy are the pure of heart," that is, the holy of heart; "they shall see God." Concretely this means that the more holy we are in spirit, the more clear we shall be in mind. We shall be able, as no one else, to recognize truth and distinguish it from error. We shall be able to see the will of God because our souls are united with the mind of God. We shall be strong to resist the seduction of sin because we are convinced, not from books but from the Spirit who dwells in our hearts, that this world is like a shadow that passes away and that only one thing matters in this life: to be in the friendship of God.

Christ
Our
Way

The theme of what I wish to say is concisely expressed in the two opening paragraphs of the *Imitation of Christ,* where we read:

"He who follows me," says Christ our Savior, "walks not in darkness, for he will have the light of life." These are the words of our Lord Jesus Christ, and by them we are admonished to follow His teachings and His manner of living, if we would truly be enlightened and delivered from all blindness of heart.

Let all the study of our heart be from now on to have our meditation fixed wholly on the life of Christ, for His holy teachings are of more virtue and strength than the words of all the angels and saints. And the person who, through grace, has the inner eye of his soul opened to really seeing the Gospels of Christ will find in them hidden manna.

No doubt we have read these words of the *Imitation* many times, but they cannot be reflected on too often because they contain, in substance, the secret of sanctity for us sinners. They tell us what we so much need to know: that Christ is our only true way to the Father; that all other guides are as trustworthy as they are animated by His Spirit; and that apart from Him we cannot be sanctified, indeed, cannot even be saved.

WE SINNERS

The place to begin our meditation on the role of Christ in our lives is to convince ourselves of our sinfulness. Needless to say, this is not a popular notion these days, when the very mention of sin is treated by so many with condescending pity as though anyone who still talks about sin is living in the Middle Ages and has not yet caught up with the times.

Yet any authentic following of Christ begins with the admission of our own sinfulness several times over.

We are sinners because we have been conceived and born in sin. The Psalmist speaks for all of us when he tells God, "You know I was born guilty, a sinner from the moment of conception." So we have been. As children of a fallen ancestor, we come into the world laden with a nature that is estranged from its Creator.

Of course, once baptized, we recover the state of grace that Adam lost for his progeny. But justification through baptism does not remove those terrible effects of sin we call concupiscence. We have within us a host of maddening drives—to lust and pride, to envy and avarice, to anger and sloth, and to gluttony—that no amount of romanticism about being "captains of our souls" can nullify.

These drives are not, of themselves, sins, and resisted with God's grace they are the source of great merit. But they can lead to sin as they are the result of sin. With St. Paul they more than once force us to say that we are prone to do what we will not, and tend not to want to do what we should. Sin as sinfulness is our common human lot, from which faith tells us that only Christ and His Blessed Mother were exempt. The rest of us daily recite the invocation, "Holy Mary, Mother of God, pray for us sinners," because we are so desperately in need of assistance to cope with our sinful urges and fears.

We are sinners, too, because we have personally offended the Divine Majesty by our acts of disloyalty and our willful resistance to grace. Think back to the earliest days of our age of reason, which is more properly called the age of discretion. How many times we failed in doing what already our young conscience told us was wrong!

Then go on through the years since then up to now. Certainly we have done much good and, with divine help, have practiced not a few virtues. But if we compare what we have done with what we should have done, the disparity is so great that, in the language of the saints, we are overwhelmed with our ingratitude to the good God and all but crushed with the realization that we have failed Him who has given us all that we have and who wants only our heart in return.

Finally, we are sinners because we have come into a world populated by sinful people. From the moment of entering human society, we have been surrounded by the example of people who ignore the laws of God and, as we are now seeing, people who create their own laws of State in contradiction to the most sacred precepts of the Almighty.

We are sinners, therefore, by nature and by conduct and by environment, and the more clearly and deeply we realize this fact the more meaningful Christ will become in our lives. His name, Jesus, means Savior, as the Gospels tell us. But this name has meaning only because we know from experience that we are sinners who need to be saved.

WE NEED EXPIATION

Since we are sinners, we need to expiate the sins that have been committed, beginning with the corporate reparation that has been going on since the fall of our first parents and penetrating every facet of our personal lives.

This word "expiation" deserves some explanation. We commonly associate the term with making reparation for an injury, or atoning for a sin, or suffering punishment for an offense or crime. All of these ideas are correct, but of themselves they do not identify exactly what we do when we expiate.

We do two things, or either one of them. We make up to God for having offended Him by loving Him more than we would have had we not sinned; and we deprive ourselves of what we have a right to in order to undo the injustice we committed by indulging the passion or the creature preference we did not have a right to.

To impress ourselves with the import of the first meaning of expiation, that is, loving God more since we have sinned than we would have had we not sinned, it is worth briefly recalling the episode described by St. Luke about the sinful woman who showed what seemed to be such extravagant repentance at the feet of Jesus. After Christ had rebuked Simon the Pharisee for his lack of courtesy and his self-righteous indignation at the woman's emotional behavior, the Savior told him what we also need to hear: "'I tell you, that...her many sins are forgiven — because of her great love. Little is forgiven the one whose love is small.' He said to her then, 'Your sins are forgiven'" (Lk. 7:47-48).

We expiate our sin by loving God more than we might have had we not come to recognize our sinfulness.

No doubt, absolutely speaking, the degree or intensity of our love for Him is determined by His infusion of grace. Our Lady never sinned, and yet she loved God with more fervor than any repentant sinner ever could. This needs to be noted lest we get the wrong idea that the way to grow in the love of God is first to sin greatly, as though repentance is the only way to sanctity. Not so.

Having said this, however, it is also part of God's providence to permit sin in the world in order that mysteriously the sinner's sorrow for having offended God will draw him closer to his Maker than might otherwise have occurred.

We further expiate sin by practicing what we call mortification, which is a good Catholic word that should be brought back into our daily vocabulary. Mortification is not some exotic form of self-flagellation that clever writers delight in exposing to ridicule. It is the conscious and deliberate depriving of myself of something that is not wrong, in order to repair for the indulgence of myself in something that was wrong. Another way of describing mortification is to call it, "Saying 'No' to certain legitimate natural pleasures because I had previously said 'Yes' to certain illegitimate satisfactions of body or mind."

Viewed in this light, mortification is a very supernatural thing. Human instinct elevated by grace spontaneously senses the need for undoing what was done wrong, and there is no more harmful attitude to adopt for us Christians than to suppose that somehow mortification has become passé. What stupidity! As though suddenly after two thousand years of Christian experience the law of reparation had ceased. Certainly sin has not become less sinful with the passing of time. It can only be because some overly educated sinners have decided to rationalize their sinfulness and are now trying to deceive others by their own self-deceit.

WE NEED CHRIST THE SAVIOR

All that has been said so far is part of our faith, which identifies us as sinners and postulates on our part the practice of expiation twice over: once by intensifying our love in reparation to an offended God, and once again by denying ourselves such creatures as divine grace inspires us to "give up" to undo the harm caused by our own sins and those of others who, like us, have added to the storehouse of iniquity in the human race.

At this point, it would be customary to speak of the saving merits of Christ, who by His passion and death has redeemed us from sin and saved us for a blessed eternity. The approach is correct, and too much cannot be made of the need we have of Christ's merciful grace to us poor sinners. St. Paul's letter to the Romans has become the Church's magna charta of deliverance for a sinful humanity.

"...the love of God has been poured out in our hearts through the Holy Spirit who has been given to us. At the appointed time, when we were still powerless, Christ died for us godless men. It is rare that anyone should lay down his life for a just man, though it is barely possible that for a good man someone may have the courage to die. It is precisely in this that God proves his love for us: that while we were still sinners, Christ died for us" (Rom. 5:5-8).

"Now that we have been justified by his blood, it is all the more certain that we shall be saved by him from God's wrath. For if, when we were God's enemies, we were reconciled to him by the death of his Son, it is all the more certain that we who have been reconciled will be saved by his life. Not only that; we go so far as to make God our boast through our Lord Jesus Christ, through whom we have now received reconciliation" (Rom 5:9-11).

It is in this sense that Christ is our Truth and our Life. He is our Truth because He has revealed the saving truth of our reconciliation by His blood. He is also our Life because the grace He merited on the cross is the life by which our souls are animated and pulsate with a share in the very life of God.

But Christ is also our Way. And this introduces a different dimension to our need of Him that many people commonly advert to. What are we saying?

We affirm that Christ is our Savior not only as the cause of our salvation by winning our reconciliation with the Father. He is also our Savior by giving us the example of expiation for sin that makes Him the perfect model for us to imitate. He is literally the Way that we are to follow in expiating sin.

But immediately an important proviso must be made. When we say that Christ is our pattern of expiation, we do not mean that He had to expiate for His own sins. He was the innocent Lamb of God, yet, as John the Baptist promptly added, "who takes away the sins of the world."

What this means is that we are to follow Christ in His attitude toward sin, in His abhorrence of sin, in His patient endurance of the sinful deeds of others, and in His suffering in sacrifice for sin. Each element in this quadrad is a cluster of mysteries that we can only glance at and then ask the Savior to better understand and put into practice.

Christ's attitude toward sin is best seen in the constant theme of His preaching, in which He preached repentance for sin and conversion from sinful attachment to creatures. There could be no compromise between serving God and mammon; anyone who was not with Christ was against Him; and on the last day, the human family would be judged on its obedience to the divine commandment of loving one's neighbor even as Christ has loved us.

"Go away from me, with your curse upon you, to the eternal fire prepared for the devil and his angels," is what the gentle Savior of the world will pronouce on unrepentant sinners. Human language could not be more terrifying, and God wants us to be terrified at the prospect of eternal fire as the recompense for unforgiven, because unrepented, sin.

Christ's abhorrence of sin is thus perfectly revealed in the final judgment and no amount of rhetoric or theological speculation can remove the simple truth of our faith: God hates sin. Certainly He loves the sinner and is divinely merciful toward the humble who acknowledge their sinfulness. But a day will come when mercy will cease and divine justice will take over.

The lesson for us is clear. If we are to imitate Christ in His abhorrence of sin we must abhor it. Nothing less. When we abhor something, we hate it, we loathe it, we detest it. To abhor is to stay away from, to have a feeling of revulsion toward what we abhor.

This gives us room for a long, long pause. Let us examine our hearts and ask ourselves how sincerely we can say that we truly abhor what we know, on faith, is sinful and that God wants us to eradicate from our lives. The measure of our abhorrence of sin is the index of our imitation of Christ.

Part of the mystery of Christ the Savior is the patient endurance of sin on the part of others that formed almost the web of His earthly life.

Think of all that happened in His public life, transmitting the savage attempt on His life almost as soon as He was born.

St. Luke opens the account of Christ's preaching at Nazareth by giving us this example of opposition which He met in His own home town:

"At these words the whole audience in the synagogue was filled with indignation. They rose up and expelled him from the town, leading him to the brow of the hill on which it was built and intending to hurl him over the edge. But he went straight through their midst and walked away" (Lk. 4:28-30).

That was the beginning of Christ's ministry. His first appearance among His own people and the same day they became enraged at His message. They took hold of Him and were ready to kill Him before He had even started.

Follow the Savior from that day to the day of His crucifixion on Calvary. All through His journeys from one town to another, sinful men caused Him untold anguish. They mocked Him and called Him dirty names; they laughed at Him, and the leaders tried everything in their power to tear down His prestige. They hounded Him from one place to another, tried to stone Him. Many who had been His disciples left Him, and finally His enemies bribed one of His apostles to betray the Master. Then they accused Him falsely, and the rest of their cruelty is the bloody narrative of the passion.

When we talk about the imitation of Christ, let us not overlook this essential feature of

His character: His patient suffering at the hands
of sinful men. Otherwise we run the risk of
imitating the wrong Christ and of modeling our
lives on a creation of our fancy. This Jesus whom
we are bidden to follow is a suffering Jesus,
whose suffering was inflicted by the envy and
malice, the cowardice and treachery of sinners.
Any other estimate of the Savior is pious fiction;
it is not the stark reality of the Gospels.

How we need that lesson in our day, when
those who would be true to the Savior are called
upon to suffer, like Him, at the hands and lips
and pen and silence and cutting remarks of
those who are either unbelievers or (may God
forgive them) Christians who have produced a
Christ of their own making and resent anyone
who still insists that the Christ of yesterday is
the same today and forever.

But that is not all. Christ is Jesus, which
means Savior, precisely because He sanctified
the sufferings He endured by making them
sacrifices, pleasing to the heavenly Father and
expiatory of the sins of mankind.

This is the main lesson we are to learn from
Christ's teaching us the way of salvation and,
beyond salvation, of sanctification. What is
this Way? It is the Way of the Cross whereby
we not only patiently suffer what God's providence sends us but actually welcome the
cross into our lives because on it was crucified
the one we love as our God.

How does sacrifice differ
from suffering? In many ways, but in none
more surely than in the readiness with which we
embrace whatever pain the Lord sends us. This

readiness to be assimilated to Jesus is the mark of a true follower of the Savior. He suffered humiliation and disgrace, and underwent such persecution as only God suffering at the hands of His creatures could endure. We become more like Him the more readily and, let me say it, gladly we accept whatever He either places into our lives or asks us to undergo for love of Him.

This kind of dialect not everyone understands. It is, in fact, a strange tongue to anyone who does not believe. But to those whom grace has enlightened, it is profound wisdom because it reveals hidden depths of meaning that are closed to those who do not believe.

We who have the faith know that pain is not useless and that suffering is not wasted pain. Provided we receive the suffering in the spirit in which God sends it, we shall unite our endurance with that of Christ. Together with Him we contribute to the world's salvation, beginning with our own; and in the company of our crucified Redeemer we advance the world's sanctification, again beginning with our own.

For all of this we need much light and strength: light to see that all of this *is* true, that it is not make-believe; and strength to bear with what the Lord gives us that costs us, without either complaint or fear. Why complain? This is the way that leads to heaven. Why fear? He is with us, indeed within us, who told us, "Do not be afraid, I have overcome the world."

Christ
Our
Light

In his address for the opening of the Holy Year for 1975, Pope Paul VI said something that must have seemed odd to many people. He stressed the need especially for a renewal of faith among the faithful during the Jubilee Year of renewal and reconciliation. What makes this seem strange is the fact that all the emphasis in religious circles these days is on love or social involvement. It certainly is not on faith.

Yet the Pope said what he did because he knows, better than other people, that true renewal of spirit among believers either begins with a renewal in what they believe or it is renewal only in name. Consequently, it is not only not surprising but should be obvious that what the Church first needs today is for her members to deepen and clarify and strengthen their faith convictions. If their faith is what it

should be, all else has the promise of a true
renascence in piety and the service of one's
neighbor. But if their faith remains weak or
confused, or contaminated with error, the bright
promise of a reformation in the Catholic Church
will turn out to be a dream or, worse still, a de-
ceptive mirage.

My purpose here is to look at
just one aspect, although a fundamental one, of
this renewal of faith that the Vicar of Christ is
urging upon the faithful. We shall look at the
person of Christ, who is our Light, and ask
ourselves these questions:

1. What does it mean when we say that
Christ is the Light of the world?

2. How is it that so many people prefer the
darkness to the Light which is Christ?

3. How can we distinguish between what
is the light of Christ and what is the darkness
that is not from Christ?

4. What implications does this have for the
renewal of spirit to which we are specially called
in the spiritual life?

THE LIGHT OF THE WORLD

It is especially in St. John's
Gospel that Christ is identified as the Light
which enlightens every man that comes into
this world. His followers are told to walk in
this light so that they may be free, and without this light all is darkness and spiritual night.

So we ask, "How is Jesus the Savior also,
and necessarily, our Light?" This is not an un-
important question in our day when there is

so much confusion among Catholics, including not a few priests and religious.

If there was ever an age in the Church's history when the faithful needed the light of Christ's direction and guidance, it is our age. Theories and theologies on every conceivable issue, conflicts and controversies on all sides— until the head reels with dizziness on even some of the most fundamental positions of Catholic Christianity. Surely today, if ever, we need Christ the Light to save us from the fog of uncertainty that surrounds us on every side.

How is Christ the light of the believing soul? He is our light insofar as He has revealed to us, through the Church, those mysteries which until His time had been hidden from the beginning of the world.

What are we saying? We are saying that the Light of Christ is the Light that is Christ. His revelation of Himself to us is the knowledge that we cannot do without if we are to see what life is all about, what suffering is all about, what death is all about, and what life after death is all about.

It is remarkable how apparently wise unbelievers can seem. They are often so naturally brilliant, so educated, and so glib in their speech that we can be taken off guard.

Think of how respectfully our modern world looks upon men and women who have received professional degrees in some field like psychology or sociology, and how apologetic the average American is for not having gone to college. We have made a fetish of native intelligence and an idol of mental education, until people assume that if a person has the brains and the training he is, if not infallible, at least the most trustworthy to know the right answers to any questions raised by the human mind.

The last thing most people ask about an intelligent, well-educated person is whether he is a believing Christian.

Yet that is what mainly makes the difference. No matter how otherwise clever a person may be, or what his academic training, unless he shares in the revelation that Christ brought into the world, he is living in darkness and, as St. John tells us, "in the shadow of death."

This deserves to be emphasized because we are so naturally prone to think differently. It takes no small amount of insight and, I would add, courage to recognize greater wisdom in a believing child of ten than in a learned agnostic of forty.

Yet, the truth is that when Christ dwells by faith in a soul, neither chronological age, nor intellectual ability, nor scholastic education really matter. His light confers on the one who believes such understanding of God and the things of God as nothing else can supply for.

WHY IS DARKNESS PREFERRED?

John the Evangelist said of Christ's contemporaries that they preferred the darkness to the light that Christ came to give to the world. Actually John was speaking for every age since then, and not only for first-century Palestine.

There is a curious twist in human nature that defies rational analysis, in that so many people literally prefer error to the truth and then glory in their preference, as though they had found a great treasure.

Why should this be so? No one but God fully understands. But at least we know something of an explanation that can help us escape the same fate.

The explanation lies in the fact that accepting Christ makes considerable demands on man's love of independence, on his desire for pleasure and ease, and on his natural dread of humiliation and pain.

Reflect for a moment on some of the leading themes of the Savior's teaching:

— Love your enemies. Do good to those who hate you.

— Lend and do not expect to receive in return.

— If a man even so much as looks at a woman lustfully, he has already committed adultery with her in his heart.

— If they have persecuted me, they will also persecute you.

— If your eye scandalizes you, pluck it out. If your hand or your foot scandalizes you, cut it off. It is better to enter the kingdom of heaven with one eye, or with one hand or foot, than with two eyes or hands or feet to be buried in hell.

— Deny yourself, take up your cross daily, and follow me.

— He that loves his life shall lose it. And he that loses his life for my sake and the Gospel shall find it.

So the litany of sacrifice could go on. From beginning to end, the Gospels are a mosaic of quotable passages, one more demanding than the next. Taken together they are a formidable obstacle to our selfishness and a veritable mountain to climb in the following of Christ.

Is it any wonder, then, that so many people prefer falsehood to the truth? What happens is not what seems to happen. It is not so much that people literally choose the untruth, as untruth, or that they particularly relish a lie. No, it is rather that they prefer the self-gratification that what is untrue before God brings to their lives.

Take the simple fact of chastity. Christ is too clear on the purity He expects of those who call themselves His disciples to leave any doubt of His expectations.

On the other hand, what Christians call unchastity but the world calls the pleasures of sex offers too much bodily (and emotional) satisfaction to be ignored. So the untruth of unchastity is embraced not because it is untrue but, though untrue, because it is so pleasant.

DISCERNMENT

We hear a great deal these days about the discernment of spirits. And well we might because there is great need for supernatural prudence to distinguish between what is truly Christian and Catholic, and what only pretends to be either or both.

With all this preoccupation, however, with discernment it is imperative that we keep things simple and not get lost in theological speculation.

The plain question is: How can we, practically speaking, know the difference between an inspiration from Christ and a temptation from the antichrist?

A good rule of thumb is to ask what side of our nature the impulse favors. Does it favor self-will or does it favor self-sacrifice? If it favors self-will, we can be sure the impulse is not from God, because self-will is another name for pride. If it favors self-sacrifice, we can be equally sure the impulse is from God, because self-sacrifice is another name for humility — and humility is certainly the sign of the presence of the Lord.

This simple rule is more useful than may appear on the surface. How many times a week and, for some of us, a day, we are conscious of contrary movements battling for the mastery of our souls. These movements take on countless different forms and they are almost infinite in variety.

We ask ourselves, I wonder if this feeling is a good one? Should I resist it or give in to it? I wonder if this idea is a sound one? Does God want me to follow it or ignore it? How can I tell?

So we return to what we had just said before. We apply the norm of self-will or self-sacrifice, and we cannot go wrong. At the heart of Christ's teaching to His followers is the message He gave us, namely, the doctrine of humble self-denial. He invariably leads those whom He is drawing to Himself by inspiring them to love His will more than their own, in a word, to die to themselves in the performance of what He wants them to do.

IMPLICATIONS

Having said all of this, however, we still have some implications to see — not the least of which is the problem of carrying into effect what our faith tells us is true.

This is where our trust in God becomes so necessary. For it is one thing to believe that Christ wants us to be like Him in meekness and humility of heart. It is something else to believe it so firmly that we act on our faith and then learn from experience how true this belief really is.

That is the secret. Christ is our Light because He truly enlightens. If we follow His illuminations we shall find out for ourselves how wise we shall become. We shall discover that being little in our own eyes is the greatest wisdom we can acquire. We shall grow in that deepest of all knowledge: that humility of heart produces peace of heart, and peace of heart gives joy to the heart — such as only Christ can give.

It is up to us to take the Savior at His word. The saints took Him literally. That is why they became saints, that is, persons who did not allow Self to stand in the way of Christ's light. His light gave them life, the life that is open to everyone who loves God more than himself and is willing to be despised in order that, through him, God might be glorified.

Christ Our Strength

We do not normally think of Christ or speak of Him as our strength. More frequently we refer to Him in the terms He used of Himself when He said He was the Way, the Truth and the Life. Moreover, we usually ask our Lord to give us strength, but we seldom think of Him precisely as not only giving us strength, but as being our strength.

What, then, do we mean when we talk about the Savior as literally the strength on which we rely and without which—better, without whom—we would be unequal to the trials of life?

We mean many things, but especially two. Christ is the strength of our minds; and He is the strength of our wills, as we struggle with our weakness and so often seem to be all but crushed by the burdens that the providence of God places on our shoulders to bear.

73

CHRIST THE STRENGTH OF OUR MINDS

We speak correctly of having a strong mind, by which we mean that some people have deep convictions about things in which they firmly believe. They are absolutely certain that certain things are true, and that other things are untrue. And we all admire such people, provided their convictions are strong about the right things, and they are unwavering in their certitude about the truth.

This is where Christ is indispensable for His followers, and so desperately important in this age of massive confusion. His presence in our souls by His grace affords us, if only we are willing to let Him act within us, absolute certitude that He *is* the Truth, that He *is* the Light, that He *is* the Wisdom of God in human form, and that apart from Him all is a jungle of darkness and the blackness of starless night.

At this point, we could correctly speak of the sure guidance that Christ's words, recorded in the Gospels, assure those who believe in Him. And it is impossible to exaggerate the need for daily meditation on the life of Christ, to give us the strength we need to know what God wants us to do, since He came down on earth to teach us as a member of our human family.

But there is another role, less adverted to, that Christ plays as the strength of our minds. According to His promise at the Last Supper, as recorded by John, He dwells in the depths of our souls, which means in the recesses of our minds, by the Spirit (His Spirit) whom we received at Baptism and who was more abundantly infused in us in the sacrament of Confirmation.

What are we saying? We are saying that Christ by His Spirit lives within us, that He is here in the inner sanctum of our intellects, interpenetrating our faculty of knowledge in a way that beggars description but is no less true for being a mystery that we cannot fully understand.

Very close, therefore, is our Teacher — right inside the minds with which we think. We do the thinking, indeed, but He is there in the classroom of our spirit, teaching us what we need to know. He is telling us, better than any book or merely human pedagogue could ever instruct us. And all He asks of us is that we believe in Him. Remember what He told us, "I am the light of the world. No follower of mine shall ever walk in darkness" (Jn. 8:12). Having come into the world, He has remained in the world. And what is so comforting to know, He is in the world of our own inner consciousness, teaching us the truth, if only the ears of our spirit are attuned to listen to Him.

CHRIST THE STRENGTH OF OUR WILLS

But the Savior is not only the strength of our minds by the wisdom He infuses into these dull intellects of ours. He is also the strength of our wills that are so vacillating and fearful, so in need of courage to face the responsibilities of our state of life. Another word for this strength of will is courage.

Too often, I think, we look on courage as having to do with undertaking a new enterprise, or facing impending danger, or pioneering in some work that no one else has tried. No doubt it does take courage to plunge headlong but not rashly into something that we foresee involves a great risk.

But the courage of the Gospels, and the one meant specially for the disciples of Christ, is the virtue of endurance. Christian fortitude, therefore, is more an affair of repressing fears than of moderating rashness. The principal act of courage, as we understand it, is to endure and withstand difficulties firmly, rather than to attack them.

As we reread the message of the Savior in this light, we see how important it is to understand what He meant by those frequent exhortations to courage:

"I say to you who are my friends: Do not be afraid of those who kill the body and can do no more" (Lk. 12:4).

"So do not be afraid of anything. You are worth more than an entire flock of sparrows" (Mt. 10:31).

"Do not live in fear, little flock. It has pleased your Father to give you the kingdom" (Lk 12:32).

"You will be hated by all on account of me. ...Nothing is concealed that will not be revealed, and nothing hidden that will not become known" (Mt. 10:22; 10:26).

"Do not let your hearts be troubled. Have faith in God and faith in me" (Jn. 14:1).

"I tell you all this that in me you may find peace. You will suffer in the world. But take courage! I have overcome the world" (Jn. 16:33).

Why, we ask, does Christ so often remind us to be brave, not to falter, to be courageous? Because He knew that our greatest obstacle to serving Him as we should is fear—fear of the opposition that loyalty to Jesus always brings in its wake; fear of the indifference of those whom we have come to love, or, as Christ put it, the enemies in our own household; and above all, fear of ourselves, whom we know all too well and by whom we have been so often betrayed.

We need the courage that comes from Christ and, indeed, in Christ, if we are to successfully conquer these inveterate fears.

What is He telling us? He is saying that just as He dwells in our minds to enlighten them and give them true wisdom, so He dwells in our wills to strengthen them and give them the fortitude that, of ourselves, we do not have.

Recall the parting message to the disciples before He ascended into heaven: "...I send down upon you the promise of my Father. Remain here in the city until you are clothed with power from on high" (Lk. 24:49). And again, "You will receive power when the Holy Spirit comes down on you; then you are to be my witnesses in Jerusalem, throughout Judea and Samaria, yes, even to the ends of the earth" (Acts 1:8).

After He ascended into heaven, Christ sent this Spirit of power, which is His Spirit, to dwell in our hearts. And since, as God, Christ is eternally united with the Father and the Holy Spirit, it is the infinite power of God that mysteriously envelops our souls. Our wills are, to use a crude expression, wrapped up in divine power and while still remaining our own human wills, they participate in the all-powerful will of God who, by grace, makes His home in us.

IMPLICATIONS

It is one thing, however, to tell ourselves that all of this is true. It is something more to also act on our belief and make the divine indwelling an effective mystery in our lives. How can we rise above merely believing that the power of Christ abides in our souls to putting the fact into practice?

My first recommendation is best expressed in St. Paul's declaration that he actually gloried in his infirmities. By this he meant something which takes a long time for most people to learn: it is the fact that our failures and weaknesses are God's way of arousing us to rely more and more on the power that comes from Christ and less and less on the strength that we ourselves so obviously do not have.

There is more here than we may suspect. It is possible we have become so conditioned to look for improvement in our moral lives that when clear evidence of it is lacking, we get discouraged at our notorious failure to live up to the high expectations we have (or had) about our spiritual potential. "Look at me," we say to ourselves, "here I am, twenty, thirty, or more years in the priesthood, or the religious life, or marriage, and I must honestly confess I am no better than I was two decades ago. If anything, I am more irritable, less patient, more selfish, less understanding than I know I was when, say, I first married or entered the postulancy."

Before saying anything else, let me be clear in repeating what the Church teaches us: God is the true judge of our spiritual vitality—not we ourselves. Consequently how *we* think of ourselves is not important. It is God's estimate that matters, not our own subjective and necessarily prejudiced opinion.

Having said this, however, let me go on. Let me insist with all the emphasis possible that God has a providentially fundamental purpose in allowing us to see our moral weaknesses and our apparent inability to overcome certain faults of character.

He knows better than we how prone we are to pride. I do not necessarily mean the pride of a domineering personality that considers itself, like the Pharisee, superior to others or goes around boasting of its achievements and belittling the efforts of others. I mean the pride of complacency that blindly fails to give credit where credit is due, namely to God, for whatever virtue we possess, and that stupidly forgets to praise the divine goodness for whatever moral goodness we may have.

So what does God do? To make sure we remain spiritually humble and to protect us from our own folly, He permits our failures to plague us, maybe to our dying day. He wants to keep us, moreover, constantly aware of our need of Him, which concretely means constantly in touch with Him by prayer.

True enough, He could not be closer to us. His nearness to us is beyond description. No human person is as near to his friend, no wife to her husband, and no child to its mother—even in the womb—as our God is to us.

But God's closeness to us is no guarantee of our closeness to Him. We can forget Him, be unmindful of Him and, in fact, ignore Him without whose presence we would not even exist, let alone do anything worthwhile on the path to eternal glory.

So, in order to make sure we do not forget Him, He permits our human nature to assert itself. He lets us make fools of ourselves, in order to have us turn to Him in frequent, childlike prayer, telling Him, "Lord, You know me and You probe me. You know how helpless I am without You and how much I need You."

We are humiliated in our own eyes, which is healthy, and we discover what only the humble of heart can learn: that the foolishness of men is the wisdom of God and the littleness of men is the greatness of God.

Then, what used to be, perhaps, only beautiful passages in the Scriptures, become filled with meaning. Then we are ready to say, and know from experience how true it is, that when I am weak, then I am strong because of the strength of Christ who abides in me.

Peace
of
Heart

There is no need to explain why we should talk about peace of heart. If there is any single recommendation, and even mandate, that His followers received from Christ, it was to be at peace.

Before the birth of Christ, Zechariah, the father of John the Baptist, was filled with the Holy Spirit to prophesy the Benedictus, which he concluded with the promise that "the rising Sun will visit us, to guide our feet into the way of peace."

When Christ was born at Bethlehem, the angels sang the first *Gloria in excelsis* with the promise again of "peace to men who enjoy God's favor."

During His public life, when Christ forgave sinners and healed the sick, He told them to go in peace.

Before His passion, when the Savior wept over Jerusalem, He was overcome with sorrow because its inhabitants did not heed "the things that are to your peace." And at the Last Supper, Jesus told the disciples (and through them He was telling us what we are so prone to forget):

"Do not let your hearts be troubled. Trust in God, and trust in me."

"Peace I bequeath to you, my own peace I give you, a peace the world cannot give, this is my gift to you. Do not let your hearts be troubled or afraid" (Jn. 14:1, 27).

Then, on the evening of His resurrection from the dead, Christ's first word to the frightened apostles was the command, "Peace be with you," which He repeated: "Peace be with you."

True to the spirit of the Master, the apostles, especially St. Paul, never tired of telling the faithful to be at peace. And finally, in the opening verses of the last book of the Bible, John pronounces the invocation, "Grace and peace to you from him who is, who was, and who is to come," that is, from Jesus Christ.

So the theme goes on, and so the Church in her liturgy keeps praying to the Lord to give us peace. And so the heart of man keeps hungering and searching for that peace which Christ promised to those who serve Him.

Now we ask: If peace of soul is such a precious commodity, is it inevitable for those who believe in God, or do we have to strive to achieve it?

There seems to be no need to say what everyone knows only too well. Peace is not automatic even with the possession of faith

or, for that matter, with the possession of considerable virtue. Peace must be achieved to be acquired. It is the fruit of grace, no doubt, but also and very much the result of our co-operation with the grace we receive.

KINDS OF PEACE

Before we look more closely at the kind of peace we are mainly concerned with, it may be useful to place it in context by seeing what different kinds of peace there are.

There are, in general, two kinds of peace that, for want of better terms, we call external and internal.

External peace is outside of us and has to do with harmony between people. Thus when two or more nations cooperate with one another and are not at war, we say they are at peace. When different classes of people, having different religions, or different languages and cultures, or different races and colors work together without conflict, we say they are at peace. And when individuals, like husband and wife, or parents and children, or brothers and sisters, relatives and neighbors, respect one another and get along together, again we say they are living in peace.

Internal peace is different. Here the absence of conflict and the presence of tranquillity are inside of us. Thus we are at peace with God when our hearts do not reproach us for being in sin or at odds with His known will in our regard. We are interiorly at peace with others when we hold no grudge against them, no ill feeling or enmity, and when they do not disturb us. We are finally at peace with ourselves when the two parts of our being, the higher and the lower, are in harmony; when our desires do not exceed our needs; when our passions are responsive to reason and our freedom is in control; when our conduct agrees with our conscience and our conscience is totally subject to God.

Among these different kinds of peace, it is clear that some are more primary than others and that there is, as it were, a hierarchy of importance in the peace that we possess and correspondingly there is a scale of priorities to cultivate if we wish to not only hear or read about peace, but be at peace as God and His Church want us to be.

External peace is the effect of internal peace. Without the one, the other is impossible. There cannot be agreement between people unless there is first tranquillity within people. We project what we are, and we produce only what we personally have. If we are at peace within, we shall be at peace with others; no more and no less. Hence the first conclusion we may draw from our reflections so far: Be at peace inside your own heart; otherwise, you will never be truly at peace with others or, what is less obvious, they cannot be with you.

Peaceful people are peaceable people. People who are in conflict in their own hearts are in conflict with others, no matter how well they may try to disguise the fact, or how negatively quiet their interpersonal relations may seem to be. After all, peace is not merely the absence of conflict. Otherwise two pieces of stone would be at peace, whereas they are only two lumps of inert matter that happen to be near each other. True peace is eminently positive;

it is an active harmony between two or more people who work together in the spirit of Christian charity.

Internal peace, then, is the cause of all external peace among nations as within families or communities, whether secular or religious. It is also the unique source of peace within the Catholic Church. So much so that we can say without fear of contradiction that the main cause of unrest in the Church today is the conflict within the hearts and minds of those who form the Church. Their internal unrest is the seedbed of the conflict that is now rocking the Mystical Body of Christ to its foundations.

THE WAY TO INTERIOR PEACE

Having said all of this, we still have to consider the most important area. If interior peace within us is the cause and/or condition of external peace between us, how do we achieve internal peace of soul?

I doubt if any subject of the spiritual life has been written on more often. Yet, the answer is not complicated, although putting it into practice may not be easy. Let me capsulize what I am going to say in a series of principles, which I will first state and then, in each case, briefly explain.

1. *Our fallen human nature means that we have unruly passions*. This may sound like a platitude, but it is not. The root of our inner conflicts and the battleground which we must cross to attain peace is our fallen human nature with its disorderly passions and drives.

No one, except as faith tells us for certain Christ and His mother, is exempt from this form of military service, that is, of struggling with our passionate urges that are consequences of original sin. You name the urge and we have it. Not everyone has all of them in the same degree, or to express it another way, not all of them are equally strong. Moreover, some of them may be dormant for years, and then suddenly spring up like a wild beast to try to destroy us.

With some people, the besetting passion is pride; they feel superior to other people and unwilling to admit to anyone, including themselves, that they are wrong. With some people, the dominant passion is lust; they are constantly or frequently or easily aroused to indulge their sex impulses contrary to their state of life. With some people, the strongest passion is envy; they instinctively feel sad when they see or hear of someone having what they lack or succeeding where they have only failed.

And so we could go down the litany of our maddening impulses in order to identify our own predominant ones. But there is no need. It is enough for the present to remind ourselves that we begin to acquire peace of soul once we realize that this peace is the result of victory over ourselves, which means over that part of us which is not sinful but is the result of sin and may lead to sin. With God's grace, we must battle against the forces of disintegration that are the common lot of a fallen human race.

2. *Our effort to master these passions is a large part of our labor of sanctification.* Too often, I am afraid, we picture the process of

sanctification in romantic colors, whereas its bedrock foundation is self-mastery.

This is all the more important to stress in our day when the world around us seems to have lost all sense of self-control; when self-expression is the watchword and self-denial is ignored, if not ridiculed to scorn.

I have read perhaps a hundred books and articles directed to the religious education of children, all nominally published under Catholic auspices. In only a small fraction, and they are not those commonly accepted by the religious establishment, did I find more than a token awareness of the fact that the child has a fallen human nature and that essential to its growth in Christian maturity is the effort required to overcome these sinful impulses.

For us adults the same principle of the spiritual life is true. Certainly we are to love God and our neighbor, but we shall do so only as effectively as we have struggled, and won, in our contest with the selfish desires that are deep, deep down in our inner ego.

3. *Part of this effort is the use of our minds to anticipate, to plan, and to carry out in practice what we have with His grace decided to do for God.* What am I saying? I affirm that the mastery of our passions is possible only if we use our minds. This is perfectly described by our Lord in the Sermon on the Mount in a little-known allegory. Here is what He said:

"The lamp of the body is the eye. It follows that if your eye is sound, your whole body will be filled with light. But if your eye is diseased, your whole body will be all darkness. If, then, the light in you is darkness, what darkness that will be!" (Mt. 6:23-24)

What Christ is saying is that just as the lamp of our body is the eye, without which we could not see where to go, so the lamp of the soul is our mind, without which our passions will take over.

How do we use our minds to obtain that self-mastery which is the precondition of internal peace? We do so by watching our thoughts to make sure they are those that bring us peace.

Let me take this in stages, since in practice it is so important for achieving peace of soul.

— First of all I look back. With my mind's eye I look back over the recent past, the last hour, or last half hour or day. I ask myself: what have I done which, as I now reflect on my past action, brings me peace of mind in the presence of God? I make a mental note of this action and decide it was a good action that should be repeated. Or as I reflect, I am disturbed in God's presence and decide there was something wrong about what I had done, so I decide to avoid this in the future.

— Then I look in, again with my mind's eye. I scan my present state of soul. Is it at peace in God's presence? If it is, fine. If it is not, I know something is wrong, because God wants me to be at peace. It cannot be that He is not giving me the grace. It must be that I am not sufficiently cooperating with the grace offered me. So I ask Him to let me know where I am wrong. He will tell me, provided I am ready to listen to His words.

— Finally and most critically, I look ahead. I anticipate what I am going to do and watch what happens to me while I quickly preview

my plans. Those which evoke peace in my soul
I trust are approved by God; those which cause
me disturbance or worry, I postpone for further
reflection, and if the anxiety persists, I conclude that what produced the worry by antici-
pation must not be according to the will of God.
How do I know? Because if I am sincerely
trying to do His will, I am sure *He* would not
discourage me in advance. Where peace pre-
vails, I am confident that is the direction God
wants me to go—and I go!

We have only begun to scratch the surface
of a very profound subject. It must be profound
because it partakes of the mystery of God. But
at least we should know that peace of heart is
available, in greater or less measure, as we
acquire peace of mind. And our minds will
be at peace in the degree to which they are
conformed to the mind of Christ. "Have this
mind," St. Paul tells us, "which was also in
Christ Jesus." What was the mind of Christ?
It was a mind with only one purpose: to do the
will of His Father. No self-will, no selfish
desire, no self-serving interest, no self-ad-
vantage and no self-consideration.

This is the road to peace, and there is no
other given to us to follow. We shall be as interiorly serene as our minds are set, like the
mind of Jesus, on one goal in life: to put into
practice what God asks us to do. This was the
secret of the saints. They discovered and we can
discover, too, that the petition of the Lord's
Prayer, "Thy will be done on earth as it is in
heaven," is also a promise. It is the promise
of a foretaste of heaven on earth, but only for
those who are convinced that there is no peace

in sin and no tranquillity in resisting the will
of God. Peace comes only in the practice of
virtue, which means the conquest of vice.
That is what Christ meant in His cryptic statement: "It is not peace I have come to bring,
but a sword." Yes, He came to bring peace,
but peace that must be won by the sword.

Spiritual Joy

We hear so much about the cross in Christianity that we are liable to overlook the correlative side of our faith, namely, its promise not only of peace but of positive happiness and joy.

If this aspect of our religion needed to be recognized in every age of the Church's history, it is more than ever necessary today. We are living in such personalist and subjective times, when so much value is placed on experience, that we need to stress today more than ever the assurance of personal satisfaction in living up to the demands of Christian virtue. After all, no one does anything, even a trifle, without some motive; and what better motivation for the following of Christ than the assurance of a share, already in this life, in the happiness of Christ?

THE NEW TESTAMENT
PROMISE OF HAPPINESS

It is not difficult to convince ourselves, on faith, that living up to the expectations of the Gospel carries with it the promise of joy in the service of Christ.

It all began at Bethlehem, when the angel first appeared to the shepherds watching their flock. When they saw him they were terrified. So he told them, "Do not be afraid. Listen, I bring you news of great joy, a joy to be shared by the whole people. Today in the town of David a savior has been born to you; he is Christ the Lord" (Luke 2:10-11).

It was all explained in great detail by the Savior in the Sermon on the Mount, when He taught the disciples of all future ages what we commonly call the Beatitudes but what could more literally be called the eight-fold path to happiness. In plain language, Christ assured happiness here and now, and not only in heaven later on, to all who believe in Him strongly enough to take Him at His word. The Beatitudes bring happiness infallibly, provided they are taken seriously, and put into practice literally.

Then at the Last Supper, Christ went out of His way to tell us of the joy that awaits us if only we listen to His teaching:

"If you keep my commandments, you will remain in my love, just as I have kept my Father's commandments and remain in his love. I have told you this so that my own joy may be in you and your joy be complete" (John 15:11).

St. Paul understood this well, as he so often exhorted the Christians to spiritual joy and warned them against sadness and worry of any kind. "I want you to be happy," he insisted, "always happy in the Lord. I repeat, what I want is your happiness" (Philippians 4:4).

Lest there be any misunderstanding, let us be clear that the happiness to which Christ and His apostles referred is the happiness that comes to all who follow in the footsteps of Christ.

Also to be carefully noted is that this joy is not absolute but conditional. The condition is the faithful following of Christ. If we are faithful, we shall be happy in our practice of fidelity; if we are not, we cannot expect God to keep His part of the covenant unless we keep ours. Moreover, we can institute a proportion: the more faithful we are, the more joyful we shall be, since there can be no spiritual joy without spiritual sacrifice.

HOW SPIRITUAL JOY DIFFERS FROM PEACE

Immediately, though, we come upon a difficulty. And it is not only a question of words. The problem is that the New Testament makes two kinds of promise to those who are willing to shoulder their cross. One is the assurance of peace, and the other is the reward of joy.

You might say, "What difference does it make? Give me peace or give me joy. I'm not sure I care which it is. Either one is enough for me."

But it does make a difference, and God wants us to have both, since the one is not the other, and the two together are part of our Christian patrimony.

What is peace? It is essentially the absence of discord and, when present, is a deep-souled equanimity. When we are at peace, we are not troubled or worried; we are not anxious or perturbed; we are not confused or distraught. A peaceful soul is a tranquil soul. It has been compared to a quiet sea, or a calm breeze, or the restfulness that comes after a busy day.

All these are figures of speech, but they are part of God's revealed word that He tells us we may look forward to as the reward of self-conquest of our unruly passions and fears. And as we grow in the likeness of Christ through self-immolation, we are to grow also in the peace of Christ who, as we know, had perfect self-mastery because He was the incarnate Son of God.

What is joy? It is more than peace, which it presumes, since it means the fulfillment of spiritual desires. After all, it is one thing not to have conflict; it is something more to also experience what we desire and to possess, though not perfectly, what we hope for.

We can dwell on the meaning of spiritual joy a little longer because how otherwise are we to appreciate what Christ said He would give us? The essence of joy is the experience of possessing God.

In heaven this possession will be perfect, according to the merit we gained before death. But on earth, too, we have happiness with the joy that Christ gives because we have a fore-taste of the beatific vision.

The trouble with talking about such things is that words cannot convey what they really mean. They must be experienced, or they are not known at all. The experience we are trying to describe is something like the joy that two people have just to be in each other's presence, even though words may not be exchanged. Or if words are used, it is only to reinforce the experience and deepen the pleasure of being in the company of someone we deeply love.

That is why Christ spoke of our sharing in the joy that He possesses, if, like Him, we keep the Father's commandments and remain, even as Christ does, in the Father's love. These three things go together: commandments, love, and joy. How so? If we are obedient to the Father's will, we prove our love of the Father; no less than Christ proved His love for the Father by doing His will. Love is proved by deeds. That is our side of the agreement: to want what He wants by doing what He tells us to do.

Then God comes through from His side. In return for our doing what He wants, He gives us what we need. And what do we need? By the deepest hunger of our created spirit, we are desperately in need of God. We need Him even when we do not precisely seek Him, and we desire Him even when we foolishly search for happiness where, by now, we should know it cannot be found. It cannot be found in creatures; it can only be satisfied in God.

SEEK AND YOU SHALL FIND

We still have one more question to ask ourselves: How is this happiness of spirit to be acquired, assuming that it can only be found in God?

The question is eminently practical because we assume that a person wants to do God's will and therefore has a right to expect God to come through, so to speak, with the reward He promised to those who love Him. The answer may be stated in a sentence, but its practice is not simple at all. "Live by preference, as much as possible, in the presence of God, and you will find such spiritual joy as no creature comfort or created pleasure can provide."

Notice that this practice of the presence of God is a preference. I choose freely to think of God instead of myself; and to talk with God instead of myself; and to please God rather than myself; and to rely on God more than myself; and to place the interests of God before myself. In a word, I exercise my liberty to pray to God and to turn from myself.

This training is not a locomotion through space; it is not a movement of bodily muscle or limb. It is, to use symbolic language, a raising of the heart toward the God who dwells in the depths of my soul. In either case, it means turning away from myself, not in dislike of myself but in preference for Him who is greater than I because He came before me and made me and, except for Him, I would not be.

All of this sounds like poetry except to the one who believes or better to one who knows from experience and therefore understands. But it is not poetry; it is sheer realism as the saints have so eloquently testified. Most of them did not write much about the happiness they enjoyed in doing the will of God. They did not have to. Statements like St. Alphonsus

Liguori's, "He who knows by experience how delightful it is to love God, loses all taste for earthly things," are rare. And taken out of context they seem exotic.

The acid test of realism is whether a thing works. And spiritual joy works. It produces what seem to be marvels of virtue and miracles of heroic zeal or patience or martyrdom. So they seem to be. But only on the outside. Inside the heart it is not so marvelous at all. If a person positively enjoys being patient and kind and generous and forgiving and forbearing; if he is happy to sacrifice himself and, as we say, carry the cross, then, in the words of Christ, the cross becomes light and the burden actually sweet to bear.

We close where we started, reminding ourselves that there are two sides to the imitation of Christ. There is self-denial, and there is self-transcendence. Christ foretold that the two are inseparable. The paradox of our faith is that we shall find our life, with great happiness in store for us even on this side of eternity, if we are willing to lose it for the sake of Christ and the Gospel. What it means is that we shall find God if we are willing to lose self, since the only obstacle to joy in heaven or on earth is self-will, which is the impossible attempt of a creature to find fulfillment apart from its Creator.

Our hearts were made for God, and they cannot find rest, which is peace, nor satisfaction, which is joy, except in God.

Part 2

HOLINESS
IN THE
RELIGIOUS
LIFE

Why the Religious Life? The Sanctification of the Church of Christ

Today's world is a self-conscious world. It is also a self-questioning world. This tendency toward self-analysis has understandably also affected the Church, until we now see men and women who not long ago were absolutely sure of themselves suddenly asking, "Who are we?" And they are not always able to find the right answer.

There seems no need for an apology, therefore, for raising the question of what the religious life is or, more accurately, why there is a religious life at all. The number and variety of answers being given nowadays is legion, and they are not equally persuasive. By now they fill a sizeable library of books and monographs, ranging from the bizarre to the sublime, and drawing on every conceivable source of insight or information. Some writers and speakers appeal to the social sciences for their premises, others to psychology or one of the humanities. Still others find an explanation for religious life in the Catholic Church in the pervasive custom among all religions to escape from the harsh realities of this world to silence and solitude in communion with the world beyond space and time.

Needless to say, many of those who make such reflections give us much that is worthwhile, and I would not want anything I have to say to minimize either their erudition or their scholarly findings. We can never know too much about the religious life in the Catholic Church, and human wisdom can shed much light on the meaning of this life.

Nevertheless, precisely because we are talking about religious life in the Catholic Church we must keep our balance or, from another perspective, keep our focus. This focus should be plain enough. It is the fact that, according to the teaching of the Church, religious life is not of human but of divine origin; that its foundations derive not from social or psychological need, nor even from religious fervor or instinct. They are the result of divine revelation and a religious vocation is therefore the response of divine faith.

Having said all of this, we are in a position to return to our title, which is a question and an answer. The question is: Why religious life? The answer is: Religious life exists in order to sanctify the Church of Christ. Behind this statement stands the history of so much of Catholic hagiography; the history of the holiness of Benedict and Francis and Dominic and Ignatius, of Clara and Angela and Teresa and Elizabeth Seton—and of their thousands of canonized and canonizable companions.

But our purpose is not to reflect on this history of religious saints in the Catholic Church. It is rather to take a hard look at the premises on which the Second Vatican Council based its concluding statement in *Lumen gentium,* the Dogmatic Constitution on the Church, in which men and women religious are reminded of their call to holiness:

"Let each of the faithful called to the profession of the evangelical counsels carefully see to it that they persevere and ever grow in the vocation that God has given to them. Let them do this for the increased holiness of the Church, in order to give greater glory to the one and undivided Trinity which, in and through Christ, is the fountainhead and source of all sanctity" (*Lumen gentium,*VI, 47).

The premises on which this conclusion is built are: that Christ established the Church not only as the universal sacrament of salvation but also of sanctification; that within the Church religious communities are specially called to sanctify the people of God; that they contribute to the Church's sanctification by their example, by their instruction, and by their merit of grace in the sight of God.

SACRAMENT OF SANCTIFICATION

According to her own definition of herself, "the Church is in Christ like a sacrament," that is, "as a sign and instrument both of a very closely knit union with God and of the unity of the whole human race" (*Lumen gentium,*1).

Just to clarify some vocabulary, we may note that three terms have become almost syn-

6. *Holiness in the Church*

onyms in the language of Catholicism, namely sacrament, mystery and instrumental sign.

The word "sacrament" is simply the anglicized derivative of the Latin *sacramentum,* while "mystery" is the corresponding derivative from the Greek *mysterion.* In the lexicon of theology, both mean a visible reality instituted by Christ to confer the grace it signifies. What we commonly call sacraments are the expressions of the primary sacrament of the New Law, which is the Church founded by the Son of God during His visible stay on earth.

The Church is, therefore, a sacrament because she has been established by Christ, because she is visible, and because she is an instrumental (and not merely indicative) sign that actually confers the grace she symbolizes.

Our concern is with the third of these features: the Church's effective communication of grace to mankind. That she communicates divine grace is a matter of faith. What may be less obvious is how the communication takes place. Why is this important? Because failure to see how the Church communicates divine grace is one source of failure among the Church's members — here religious — to live up to the expectations that God has of those who have been specially chosen to become instruments of grace to their fellow men.

In general, the Church can be a channel of grace to people by what she is, by what she says, and by what she does. In this she continues the salvific work of Christ whose life, words and works were the divinely effective means of communicating the blessings of the Trinity to the community of the human race.

What should be stressed, though, is that this ministry of grace from Christ through the Church is not only for the world's salvation. It is also and emphatically for the world's sanctification. What the Church is, what she says and does are intended by the Christ whose Spirit animates the Church to make people more believing, more hopeful, and more loving—in a word, to make them more holy than, absolutely speaking, they would have to be to be saved.

It is, therefore, not only to redeem the world from sin but to sanctify the world in godliness that Christ, who is the sacrament of God, came into the world and through the Church remains in our midst. The Church exists to remove sin, indeed, but not only. Her role, which is Christ's role, is to bring to fulfillment His injunction that those who believe may become perfect, even as their heavenly Father is perfect. That is why Christ "sent the Holy Spirit upon all men, that He might move them inwardly to love God with their whole heart and their whole soul, with all their mind and all their strength, and that they might love each other as Christ loves them" (*Lumen gentium*, V, 40).

If this function of the Church was always true, it is imperative today when demonic forces are at work in the world, bent on destroying the very image of God in the human heart. No ordinary goodness or mere abstention from sin is enough to cope with the dark powers that are currently so active among the children of men. Nothing but sanctity can compete with the self-idolatry that is so rampant in the world today. Only saints are a match for the devil.

VOCATION OF RELIGIOUS
TO SANCTIFICATION

At the risk of saying the self-evident, it may be worth noting that there is a difference between being holy and laboring to make others holy. It should be a commonplace that the primary call of religious is to sanctity, that is, to be holy. They will have other occupations and they can be employed in a variety of apostolic enterprises. But their vocation is to holiness. If they fail in this, they have failed in the main reason for their existence.

This is not the whole story, however, since religious have a double vocation to holiness: one for themselves and another for others. Or, from another viewpoint, their own sanctity is meant to be the instrument for sanctifying those who, through them, are to come closer to God.

For too long, I am afraid, some people have been confused about the priorities in the religious life. One reason may have been the large-scale involvement of religious in the active apostolate. In itself such involvement was laudable, and the achievements of religious in the corporal and spiritual works of mercy in our country are a standing tribute to their mighty zeal.

The trouble is that this involvement got out of hand. Men and women who may have entered the novitiate with more substantive motives in time found themselves so immersed in work—academic, social, humanitarian and service-oriented—that for many of them the universal motto of St. Benedict, *ora et labora* (pray and work), was changed into *labora et ora* (work first and, if you have the time and energy, also pray).

Do not misunderstand me. I am not saying that work cannot be sanctifying, nor that the apostolate is not of the essence of religious life. What I am saying is that it makes a great deal of difference how we define the apostolate. If it is redefined to mean that temporal welfare and human activity are primary, that human production and cerebration, or the creations of human effort are, in practice, more important than prayerful union with God, or the liturgy, or the sacraments, or self-sacrifice and bearing the cross for the love of God—then we have an inversion of what religious life as understood by fifteen centuries of Catholic Christianity is supposed to be.

The difficulty with saying this is that not a few religious who have made such an inversion would deny that they are acting on principle. They would be offended if charged with substituting what belongs to man for what belongs to God and replacing the priority of grace with the powers of human nature.

There should be no mistake about the gravity of the issues which this attitude implies. Anyone who professes the Catholic Faith can be in no doubt as to what is the main reason for Christianity; in Christ's words, our kingdom is not of this world; we have no lasting city here; we look beyond the grave to the City of God on high. Correspondingly anyone who professes the Catholic Faith should have no doubt that the means we are to use to attain heaven and the vision of God are mainly spiritual means; that human effort is mainly to be directed to predisposing ourselves for grace, to obtaining divine grace, and to cooperating with the graces received.

Religious communities, therefore, exist not to give testimony to political or social enterprises, no matter how nobly conceived. Their primary purpose, as religious communities, is to be *religious* communities. They are not to be what others are, and what they are not supposed to be — secular institutions engaged in secular pursuits. Their *raison d'être* is to witness to the efficacy of God's grace in raising fallen human nature above its native weaknesses and raising it even to the heights of sanctity, after the pattern of the first Religious, who was Jesus Christ.

But all of this presumes that religious assume that this is still their reason for being religious. They could have been educators, or nurses, or administrators, or writers, or social and political activists, without entering the religious life. And they could, in their respective professions or employments, have done good (even great) work for the benefit of society as lay people in the world.

So they could. But, in spite of a mounting literature defending the opposite, they are religious for a higher end, namely to cooperate with the Christ who called them to bring mankind closer to God in faith, hope and charity and, through the practice of prayer, humility and patience, to bring the world nearer to the purpose for which God became man and died on the cross to save.

I know how this must sound to some people. Preconciliar would be the mildest term of criticism. It is, in St. Paul's language, foolishness and a scandal because it frankly places the things of eternity above the benefits of time, and brazenly defies the values of the wise men of this world.

The world of which Christ spoke at the Last Supper may give lip service to what it vaguely calls "religion," but the secularist mind looks upon religion at worst as a distortion of reality and at best as a means to an end, that is, the good life in comfort and ease and prosperity and plenty of fuel and food and drink and a lack of physical pain and a limited family and time for leisure and recreation and not too much work and good pay. In the face of this mind set, to still talk about divinization instead of humanization, and of growth in holiness instead of progress in self-fulfillment is to invite the scorn that Christ received when He preached the incredible Beatitudes of poverty and purity and peaceableness and persecution as preconditions for the joy that only He can give to those who believe in His name.

One problem must be resolved, however, lest the mistaken impression be left that all we are saying is only a matter of emphasis.

There are those who do not see anything about religious life that is essentially different from other states of life. On these premises, religious are at most more strongly motivated lay persons. Consequently their call to holiness and their call to sanctify others are on the same plane as the corresponding vocations of other members of the Mystical Body.

If this is correct, then all the centuries of urging of the Church to religious has been misplaced. In order to clear the record, let us hear what the Second Vatican Council and Pope Paul VI have to say on the subject.

"The holiness of the Church is fostered in a special way by the observance of the evangelical counsels, proposed in the Gospels by our Lord to His disciples" (*Lumen gentium*, V, 42).

"The counsels are a divine gift, which the Church received from her Lord and which she always safeguards with the help of His grace" (*Lumen gentium*, VI, 43).

"The religious state is not an intermediate state between the clerical and lay states. But rather, the faithful of Christ are called by God from both these states of life, so that they might enjoy this particular gift in the life of the Church" (*Lumen gentium*, VI, 43).

"The Christian believer binds himself to the three afore-mentioned counsels, either by vows or by other sacred bonds that are essentially like the vows. In this way, a person is totally surrendered to God, loved above all things. It is true that through baptism he dies to sin and is consecrated to God. But that he might be able to derive more abundant fruit from this baptismal grace, he intends, by the profession of the evangelical counsels in the Church, to free himself from those obstacles which could draw him away from the fervor of charity and the perfection of divine worship. Thus he is more intimately consecrated to the divine service" (*Evangelica testificatio*, I, 7).

It is worth quoting these passages, which could be multiplied several times, to remove any vestige of doubt in today's widespread confusion: that religious life is a unique vocation that is something objectively distinctive on the part of God who gives this grace, and not merely a subjective interpretation on the part of certain people. It therefore carries with it an awesome responsibility for the consecrated religious to become holy and to labor individually and corporately for the sanctification of mankind.

SANCTIFICATION BY EXAMPLE, INSTRUCTION AND MERIT

We are now ready to ask ourselves how religious are to exercise this role of bringing others to holiness. The answer, we said, was that they are to do this by their witness of example, by their instruction of all who come under their care, and by their merit of grace for souls through the prayers and good works they perform.

Witness of Example. The first way that religious are to contribute to the sanctification of the world is by their own example of holiness, which means by their example of God-likeness, which means by their witness to the presence of the transcendent God in the midst of a fleeting and changing world. This is the way Pope Paul expressed it in his much-neglected Apostolic Exhortation to Religious:

"Today, more than ever before, the world needs men and women who are outstanding for their faith in the Word of the Lord, His resurrection and eternal life, to such an extent that they spend their entire earthly life testifying to the truth of this love which is offered to all mankind. In the course of her history, the Church has never failed to be animated and invigorated by the holiness of so many religious men and women who, following their respective form of

7. Holiness in the Church

Gospel perfection, have witnessed by their life to infinite love and to Christ the Lord" (*Evangelica testificatio,* IV, 53).

In more prosaic terms, what the Pope is telling religious is to reform their lives and become what the laity want their religious to be: men and women who witness by their lives to the truth of the Christian faith. They are to give visible testimony to the invisible mysteries of a suffering God who rose from the dead, of a cosmic struggle between Christ and the spirit of evil, of the efficacy of the sacraments and the power of prayer, of the value of sacrifice in this world, and the promise of a joy that will never end.

Instruction in the Things of God. Along with their witness of a life of above-average virtue, religious are to help sanctify the world by imitating Christ the Teacher in speaking to others of the things that are above. Behind this strange biblical image stands the promise of divine assistance to those who are not indifferent to the things that are below but who also know better than to put their hearts on earthly treasures where moths consume and rust corrodes and thieves break in and steal.

It is no coincidence but deeply significant that for more than a millennium the most influential organized body of Catholic teachers in the Church have been members of religious communities. This is only to be expected as we reflect on the fact that Christ went about preaching the Word of God. Since religious are dedicated to the imitation of the Master, they would naturally seek to do what He did. He gathered people around Him, in tens and hundreds and thousands, to tell them about the

Kingdom He was preparing for those who love Him, about the necessity of faith and the meaning of the cross, and the way to obtain mercy for sin from a forgiving God.

In our day, when so many Catholic schools are closing and others are on the way to shutting their doors, let me voice what someone must say without fear of human respect. One of the main reasons for religious life in the Catholic Church is that religious men and women might instruct the faithful in the paths of holiness. Certainly there are different ways of doing this, but none is more effective or more desired by the Church than that religious communities dedicate themselves as communities to teaching the Catholic Faith in Catholic schools that are Catholic in reality and not only in name.

Let us not be fooled by the secularist philosophy that surrounds us on every side. The children of this world are often more shrewd in this matter than the children of light. That is why modern governments are so anxious to control the school systems of their countries. They know, even if we do not, that whoever trains the youth of a nation holds the future of society in his hands. Every other factor behind the current drive for State monopoly in education is secondary to this one. It is a struggle for mastery of the human mind.

The heart of the Catholic school system in the United States, from elementary grades through the university, has been the dedication of hundreds of religious communities honestly striving to share with others something of the holiness, which is godliness, that Christ had shared with them. This school

system will survive (speaking of Sisters) where —
but only where — the dedication of an Elizabeth
Seton, a Julie Billiart, a Sophie Barat, a Catherine
McAuley still remains. It will disappear everywhere else.

Yet, there is more to this apostolate of sanctification by instruction than formal teaching
in Catholic schools, or even in confraternity
programs. It partakes of every means that religious have at their disposal to talk to people
about Jesus and Mary and Joseph, about receiv-
ing the sacraments of Penance and Holy Communion, about the Sacred Heart and the Im-
maculate Heart of Mary, about the shortness of
life on earth and the endless reaches of eternity.

Religious are to be professionals in the art
of spiritual conversation. They should be able
to speak easily and persuasively about how good
God is and how much He wants us to love Him
by loving those whom He places into our lives
for this purpose only: to show that we care for
them because we care for Him who is our
Blessed Lord and theirs.

Merit of Divine Grace. There is still one
more means and, in its way the most important,
by which religious are to be channels of sanctification. They merit graces for others by their own
life of prayer and sacrifice and the practice of
all kinds of virtue.

The doctrine of altruistic merit is not much
talked about these days. This is a pity because
it is just as true as it ever was. What it means
is that we can truly merit in the eyes of God in
the sense of effectively imploring the Divine
Majesty in favor of other persons. We can obtain
for them by our impetration graces that God
will give them not only to repent of their sins

but to become more holy, that is, more pleasing in His sight.

There is no need to dwell here on the subtle distinctions between condign merit that we can gain for ourselves and the congruous merit we gain for others. The important thing is that Catholic Christianity unqualifyingly believes in the efficacy of our prayers, works and sufferings as supernaturally beneficial to other people.

What I am saying here should be obvious, but so many of these obvious things in our faith have become obscured in our day that they need to be brought out into the open and unembarrassingly displayed for reflection. Why should this be opened up for serious re-examination? Because the activism that permeates pragmatic cultures like our own tends to underrate the interior life as an apostolic medium for saving and sanctifying souls. In fact, it runs the danger of substituting man's efforts for the grace of God. That is not the mind of the Church.

"Let no one think that by their consecration religious have become estranged from people or useless in the earthly city. For even though at times they do not directly mingle with their contemporaries, yet they are more deeply than ever close to them in the heart of Christ and cooperate with them spiritually" (*Lumen gentium*, VI, 46).

The implications of this doctrine are incalculable. The whole of a person's religious life, from the first days of the postulancy to the last hours before death, and every hour of the day are (and are meant to be) efficacious in the apostolate. Every time a religious performs an act of piety or makes a sacrifice, or offers a prayer or receives a sacrament—these are acts of religion and meritorious before God twice over: once for the religious personally and once again for others. Both kinds of merit are, of course, determined in their value by the holiness of the one who gains them and the holiness with which he or she performs the actions. What is constant, however, is the fact that God rewards what His servants do to please Him and rewards others, too, through them and, as it were, for their sakes.

This principle of sanctification by merit is equally applicable to religious engaged in what we call the active apostolate and to those devoted to a life of contemplation. It declares without reservation that, as important and even necessary as a person's external apostolic works may be, they are quite secondary to his union with God and his selfless conformity to the divine will. Indeed, the history of religious life is filled with examples of men and women who, in the Church's judgment, had done great spiritual things for the Kingdom of God although they remained hidden in the scullery or bedridden for years or, as St. Thérèse of Lisieux, the Patroness of Missions, lived all their religious life in the cloister and never preached a sermon or wrote a book or did any of those perceptible things we commonly associate with being an apostle.

The lesson for all religious should be plain. Our labors in evangelization or catechetics or the works of mercy are important in the economy of sanctification. But their fruitfulness in grace for others is to be measured not so much in terms of hours or energy or money spent, as of the degree to which the religious who spend the time and effort and resources are trying to do the will of God. Their intimacy with Him is the measure of His use of them for the advancement of His Gospel among the children of men. The sooner religious realize this fact of supernatural achievement, the better for them and for the Church and for all the People of God.

The Essentials of Religious Life

Never before in the history of the Church has the religious life been more strongly challenged, to the depths of its being.

What is being challenged today is the very essence of religious life. Religious men and women under vow are being told to identify themselves, and as they do, depending on how they formulate the identification, their very existence as religious is questioned unless they conform to certain patterns planned out for them. And if they conform, they are told they may enjoy peace and the acceptance of their fellow religious.

I propose to isolate what I consider the essentials of religious life—today, as yesterday, as tomorrow.

These essentials, I believe, are derivable first of all from the Church's unbroken tradition, from the teaching of the most solemn conclave in the Catholic Church—an ecumenical council. In all the nineteen centuries of the Church's history none has ever spoken at such length, with such depth, and in so much detail about the religious life as the Second Vatican Council. Not as much on the religious life has ever been declared in all the other twenty councils in the Church put together.

In my judgment these essentials may be reduced to six: 1) the pursuit of holiness in the following of Christ; 2) Eucharistic community life; 3) actual poverty; 4) consecrated celibacy; 5) ecclesial obedience; 6) Catholic apostolate.

Among these six, the first one—the pursuit of holiness in the following of Christ—is obviously fundamental. The second—Eucharistic community life—represents the principal means; the other four spell out both the fundamental purpose and the way these means are carried out in practice.

PURSUIT OF HOLINESS IN THE FOLLOWING OF CHRIST

In stating this as the finality of the religious life, I do not mean that a religious is to lead a merely good life (because in that sense, every Christian is bidden to follow Christ) nor to merely strive to overcome sin. Nor, of course, that he or she is to hide himself or herself away, in quiet spiritual repose—away from the maddening crowd, to work at his own religious needs.

Rather, like Christ, he is called to follow Jesus in living an intense—and the adjective to me seems to summarize everything—an intense life of prayer and charity; which means union with God and the service of one's fellowman. This dual goal of prayer and service will, of course, be differently interpreted by different institutes, but its pursuit is crucial. Nothing else may be subordinated in such a way as to imply an equality with it. It enunciates the twofold purpose of man's existence, as stated by the Savior—to love God with all our heart and to love others even as He loved us. That's the fullness of the New Law.

EUCHARISTIC COMMUNITY LIFE

As we know from the first gathering of the Church in Jerusalem, Christianity is not a solitary religion. It is either communal and societal, or it does not exist.

Consistent with Christianity as a whole, religious life—as a more intense practice of the Christian way of life—is also and necessarily communal. I would like to impress you with this. May I suggest that whatever reading and thinking you do in the future, among the elements you look for in religious life, look for this: it never thinks of itself except in terms of the community. Even the so-called solitaries in Asia were not solitaries. They were united with their fellow religious in spirit, and periodically came together, especially for reading the Scriptures and for instructing themselves in the Word of God and the Liturgy.

The religious life is a gathering of like-minded, or as I prefer, like-hearted persons who so live out their following of Christ as to be together, and work together. That being together is of the essence of religious life. Not merely working together—corporations do that. This practice of community means being together and working together as much as circumstances and the nature of the service of others allows and demands. It means living together physically whenever possible; living apart should be the exception. If it becomes the rule, it is the beginning of the end of that erstwhile religious community.

The bond of unity for religious is the common mutual love of one another, their shared concern for the welfare of others, and the united allegiance to a common authority.

But this is not all—this community life is also Eucharistic. Jesus Christ, who remains on earth in the Eucharist, forms the center of their lives, in the sacramental presence which He has among them.

The principal source of the strength of religious is the Blessed Sacrament, and the Priest who daily joins their sacrifice with His in the Eucharistic Liturgy is Jesus Christ. The history of religious life over the centuries reveals the very simple fact: where devotion to the Eucharist has been strong, religious life has flourished. Even in the early centuries, the faithful would receive Holy Communion daily. It was simply unthinkable that those who dedicated themselves under the life of the evangelical counsels would be for any length of time, or for any distance of space, far from the Eucharist. And if they could not for any reason build themselves monasteries and chapels, they would carry the Eucharist with them. Contrarily, where Eucharistic faith and worship waned, religious life weakened and finally died out. That is the law of survival.

St. Robert Bellarmine, one of my confreres, the man on whose works I spent all my spare time while studying theology and on whose work I wrote my dissertation, has over the years been my greatest inspiration after Ignatius. His observation on the sixteenth century, the revolution that shook the foundation of Christianity, that practically wiped out religious life in the northern section of Europe, in all countries, was that the main single reason for it was the neglect of the Eucharist.

ACTUAL POVERTY

As we get into the form of community life, we find that poverty is indispensable. Few aspects of the religious life are more debated—and in some quarters more debatable—than poverty. I have by now, I suppose, read through about twenty Chapter proceedings of as many religious communities. On occasion I have worked with their delegates. In every case, poverty has been the keystone problem that they face in the future. And that for a very simple reason: we are living in the United States, in the most affluent society of all human history. It is not only that there is nothing like it in other countries in the world; nothing like it has been seen—ever. No wonder poverty is a problem.

What is true religious poverty? To answer this question, we can review some of its features, all of which are valid, but none of them alone is enough—until we come to the last one. Religious poverty means a sharing of material possessions in the manner of the early Christians and certainly as the earliest religious communities practiced it. What belongs to one, belongs to all. Whether income or lodging facilities or equipment or books, or—and I can't miss the chance to say this—gifts.

Beyond sharing of material things in common, religious poverty means labor and work. It is by definition the opposite of a life of ease and luxury. Its motto is: Poverty means work; poverty means labor; poverty means exertion; poverty means fatigue. A religious gets tired—after the example of Jesus Christ. And the evangelists wanted to make sure we wouldn't miss that point. But that is not all.

Religious poverty means that a religious is dependent on the community for his needs. He does not use anything as his own and learns from experience to ask for what he wants on the prior conviction that like Christ he does not claim independent use of anything. And if his poor Master said He had nowhere to lay His head, he would have to actually, or equivalently, beg. That's what a religious should do. There are some people, even presidents of universities, who beg professionally. In community the dependence for what I need is part of religious poverty.

Let me insert here something you wouldn't ordinarily think of. For several years I taught the Oriental religions—Hinduism, Buddhism,

Islamism—and they have taught me a lot. They especially inspire me to be a better Christian, and in many ways to be a better religious. Buddhism is one of the largest monastic orders of history. Buddha was a monk; his followers are all actually or equivalently religious. Among the primary principles he laid down for his religious was that they support themselves by begging. No authentic follower of Buddha is rich. And as I look at the vast regions of China, mainly Buddhist, with their millions of people, what possible chance have we of making a Christian impact on that teeming humanity unless we learn and practice as religious our poverty, sharing alike and being dependent?

This is the main reason I say that Communism has such an easy way of conquering. It didn't conquer—it answered the ideology of the people, of a people to whom poverty is their faith; whose faith tells them to share, and whose faith tells them to depend. That's what Marxism always teaches.

Religious poverty means a poverty of spirit—a detachment of affection for material possessions and a willingness to do without. But that is not enough. Indeed, it is not enough to practice the spirit of poverty, for the very good reason that all Christians are bidden to do the same.

Authentic poverty in the religious life means actual deprivation. Not merely a willingness to be poor, but to be poor is what Christ practiced. Anyone who qualifies that is surely obscuring the teaching of the Savior. What He practiced—this is the poverty that He expects of His religious. It can scarcely be individual poverty only, as a religious, as a person; it must also be the poverty which is opposed to affluence in a community.

Sometime ago I was on a plane. By the way, when I can, I take a train or a bus, but I also fly a lot. It saves time and often money. Whatever cities I was flying between, I sat down next to a man who happened to be an architect for a large construction firm. As we began a conversation (he was not a Catholic), he said to me: "Father, could you get through to religious sisters to tell them that the buildings they put up are an architect's dream, but that they are not the kind of building that creates a good image for them in the professional world?"

CONSECRATED CELIBACY

I think the term *celibacy* is more accurate than chastity for the good reason that everyone is supposed to be chaste. Celibacy like poverty, is not merely a form of detachment, but actual practice. Religious celibacy is more than mere abstention from the privileges of marriage. A lot of women don't marry for all kinds of reasons. They're not always the reasons for consecrated celibacy.

One of the most interesting seminars I ever ran was advertised nationally as a seminar for single professional women. In three days we were somehow to come up with the major problems of single women in the world and offer them some solutions. It's one of the few weekends I didn't get ten minutes of sleep all Friday night and Saturday night. They were all around on couches, waking each other up when their turn came for the conference. And I discovered that in spite of all their success and achievement, they have problems and trials and difficulties. As I told them—and it's public knowledge—"Ladies, there is one thing you must do, or you can never be truly happy. You must accept your singlehood, (I coined the term), your singlehood as the will of God for you." That is not quite consecrated celibacy.

This celibacy of ours means more than self-control, which is implied in chastity. It is more than the virtue of temperance, by which I restrain my sexual impulses which are linked with my feelings, and hold them under control. It means dedicated love, with all the meaning that one can put into those two words—*love* and *dedicated*. The two words, *charity* and *chastity*, are not poetic alliteration. They are related as cause and effect.

Like Jesus Christ, who never married, a celibate religious dedicates his life to God in order to be more apt to give himself wholly to God in loving contemplation, and wholly to his neighbor in loving service. I would die for that statement. And we'd better believe it. Our celibacy gives us an aptitude for prayer and communion with God that others, who may be very holy and very virtuous, simply do not have. And we're the last ones to pride ourselves on the grace we've received. We also have an aptitude for serving others that those who have not so dedicated themselves do not have.

So, far from stultifying love, celibacy ennobles it, deepens it, gives it scope, freedom and a degree of openness for which there is no substitute. Every one of those words I could footnote, or better, if I had the time, could write a book on. It ennobles it, deepens it, gives it scope and expansion, freedom and an openness to the hearts of others.

Like all love, celibacy is productive. Let's never suppose for a moment that we have somehow lost our procreative power. I am too much of a man to have sanely vowed myself to celibacy unless I believed that I could reproduce myself in others. Celibacy produces, if faithfully practiced, an extraordinary union with God, but especially for our purpose, an exceptional effectiveness in serving the highest interests of others. No physical father or mother is as spiritually fruitful as a religious who lives up to his or her consecration of body and soul to Christ in celibacy.

ECCLESIAL OBEDIENCE

So many things we read and hear nowadays seem to reduce religious obedience to a typical American pragmatism. Of course, you would expect this obedience, the kind that we have undertaken, to have something useful about it. But it is far higher and deeper than maintaining good order, or furthering the self-discipline of those who practice it, or showing the effectiveness of the organization, the structure to which I belong, or certainly merely giving people a chance to co-operate with others in a common enterprise. Every good business has all kinds of cooperation in a common enterprise. Talk about rules and regulations, businesses certainly have them. That's not our obedience.

Its purpose is all of these, tempered and adjusted to the times, but it is also like the obedience of Christ—part of the mystery of redemption. The only trouble is that so much of what I have read about this "religious obedience" sometimes seems scarcely to know this dimension exists. It certainly does not stress it, and some writers—may God forgive them—even deny it. The role of religious obedience is to develop that Christian humility which God blesses with His grace and to which He attaches the promise of His special providence because that is what He practiced when He became man. We should always think of our obedience as an imitation of the great manifestation of divine obedience. Redemption is the result of obedience—from the obedience of Christ to our own. And I have lived long enough in the religious life and have dealt enough with religious of all ages and stages to be able to say this: I have seen very modest talents, simple souls, with an I.Q. just high enough to qualify for admission, doing great things for God. And I have seen, and I see, men and women of extraordinary ability who waste that talent because God will not bless conceit, pride and disobedience.

THE CATHOLIC APOSTOLATE

The essence of religious life to those who live in community is something greater than keeping busy. We all know ways of keeping busy. All of us have enough intelligence to qualify for some kind of profession, especially the profession of teaching, or performing works of social welfare. This can be done and is done as well and often better by people who are not religious. These works in themselves are not the main purpose of our religious life.

I would like to give this statistic from a diocese regarding religious women who left their communities. I know it is authentic because the man who gave it to me is the vicar of religious. They kept tab on the problems which the Sisters had before they left and what happened to them after they left. The interesting statistic is this: the ninety women who left, all after their vows, were engaged in some kind of social welfare work: inner city, race problems, etc., and ostensibly that was their reason for leaving. Yet not a single one of those ninety is now in social work.

Nor is the purpose of our religious life to raise the standards of literacy in our society or solve the problems faced by our political structure or improve the culture of America. All of these things we're involved in, some more than others. We as religious may ostensibly and really be engaged in these and other like activities, but they are neither the main purpose nor the real goal in our life. The function of religious life is mainly and ultimately and pervasively to extend the kingdom of God in the hearts and minds of men. That's it, and everything else is secondary or ancillary. Few issues of the present crisis in the religious life, especially in America, have attracted so much attention.

Everything else is secondary to the extension of Christ's kingdom and when something else becomes the preoccupation, it is irrelevant and disastrous. We are bidden by the Church to go back to the Gospel and read there what Jesus Christ did during His stay on earth and what He commissioned His apostles to do. "I have come that they may have life and have it more abundantly." He was speaking of spiritual life, the life of God in the souls and bodies of men.

In pursuit of this goal, He preached and He lived, He suffered and He died. He has invited us to share in this enterprise in the Catholic Church under His Vicar. We are to extend His kingdom to the ends of the earth — the catholicity of space. We are to teach without adulteration, in all its evangelical quality, His message, unchanged, the same that He taught in Palestine — the catholicity of time. May I suggest as a personal note that we ask our divine Savior to help us understand what He, the first religious, instituted — the religious life.

Liberty—
Choice,
Love
and Sacrifice

I suggest that we reflect on the subject of liberty in the spiritual life — the last thing I think you would expect for a meditation. I doubt if there is any single subject on which more has been written in recent years than the subject of freedom. It is, so the analysts of the Church's problems tell us, at the root of the crisis that is affecting Christianity in our day.

In popular literature and in so many of our songs, the young sing about the freedom to *be*, to be themselves, to do what they want... just to be free. Hence, the value of a meditation on freedom, the kind of freedom that God evidently wants us to practice, the freedom of the children of God.

I would like to address myself to the subject of liberty or freedom under three aspects which, if you wish, can be three points: liberty as choice, liberty as love, and liberty as sacrifice. Then, as we go along, I will make some short but, I hope, practical applications to our spiritual life.

LIBERTY AS CHOICE

The first and most obvious meaning of liberty is the ability to choose, to have options offered by the mind. And the more options the mind offers, the more free we are —which is one reason why affluent societies can be in such a crisis: there are so many options among which to choose! Freedom, then, whatever else it means, first means that I select and am not constrained to do something.

So we ask ourselves: how important is this liberty of choice for us as human beings, before we address ourselves to being religious? So important is this element of choice that it most distinctively characterizes us as human beings. What is a human being? A human being is one who has the ability to choose. This is so true that in moral theology we simply identify two adjectives: free and human. And those actions which we do not perform freely, we do not even call human. Human acts, theologically speaking, are free acts. Thus, we could redefine morality as the exercise of freedom.

But now, for us as religious, what is the highest function of this liberty of choice that we can exercise, and thereby be most pleasing to God? After all is said and done, the highest function of our freedom of choice as revealed to us by God is the freedom to choose *to pray*. Honest!

Why is this the highest and most important function? Because unless we choose to pray, no matter how gifted we may be naturally, we shall not reach our destiny. Unless we choose to pray—and we *must* choose to do so—we shall not obtain that indispensable gift of freedom which comes with grace, so that we are able to do what God wants us to do. Otherwise we shall not be saved. Those who pray will be saved; those who do not pray will not be saved. And those who pray will be holy; those who do not pray will not be holy.

Why are we so secure in saying this? Nine months, more or less, before we were born, we didn't exist. Except for God's goodness, none of us would be here. Having received so much from God without our doing anything about it—with no choice on our part to come into existence—we shall not reach the goal for which we were made unless we choose. And the first and most important exercise of this liberty is to pray and to ask for that grace which we need.

LIBERTY AS LOVE

Quite obviously, it is not enough for us merely to have the ability to choose. Important as the liberty of choice is, it is not its own ultimate purpose. We are given liberty not merely to choose, but in order that having chosen, we may love the object of our choice. This is so true that if after having chosen something, we discover sadly that we chose the wrong thing, we are not to love it. We are to make another choice and let go of the first thing we chose, so that we may not merely choose but may be able to love what we chose.

And here we ask: what is the highest object of our love? Need we say it? It is God. So if the highest function of our liberty is to choose to be in spiritual contact with God—one of my many definitions of prayer—then our highest function in loving is to love the God who made us for the sole purpose that we might love Him.

Meditations should be practical. If I meditate, and I've made a good meditation, then I do something about that on which I have meditated. A meditation which stops in the mind is speculation; it is not prayer. So how do we exercise this love of the highest object of our love, namely, our God? Let's backtrack for just a moment to get our bearings.

There is so much said and written and sung these days about love, to a point where I think in English, the word "love" should have two spellings: one, l-o-v-e, and the other, l-u-v. How do we love? Judging by so much of what the world is saying around us about love, you would think that we love with our feelings, and that the more exalted are our emotions, the more in love we are. Or, for other people, you would think that we love with our minds, and the more learned the books that we write or read on the nature of love, the more we love. No. We love with our wills.

Christ made sure that He was very plain about who *really* loves Him, and that adverb is important. A lot of people say they love, but saying they love is not the same as loving. Who, on Christ's premises, really loves Him? The one who does His will. When I do what faith and my reason tell me is God's will, I love Him, no matter what my feelings may tell me to the contrary. If I had my emotional choice, this might be the last thing I'd be doing right now. But as long as I believe this is what God wants and I do it—that's it!

Feelings don't count, and I don't mean just the negative feelings. There are certain things I do not like to do, yet if I do them because I am sure that God wants me to do them, I love Him!

"But there's no warm feeling around my heart." So there isn't. So what? "But I just read a book that said I'm to fulfill myself and that God wants me to...well, to satisfy my desires, and that I am most pleasing to God when I satisfy my own desires." That's the way some are writing lately, but they use more sophisticated words. The fact is, however, that if faith tells me God wants me to do something and I do it, in spite of negative feelings, I love Him.

The same principle holds for exalted feelings. Some people, depending on how sentimental they are (and all of us, thank God, have some sentiment), can make the mistake of somehow equating their sense of spiritual well-being—the kind of satisfaction you get after a good meal—with doing God's will, so that the more consoled they are, the more spiritual satisfaction they get and the more surely they think they are making progress in the spiritual life.

I confess I used to think so. I've learned.
Faith tells us that, as members of the Catholic
Church following a way of life approved by the
Church, whose directives have been given to
us by those whom faith tells us hold the place
of God for us, we are doing God's will and we
are loving Him. Is it any wonder that religious
life is such a sure way to sanctity, provided it is
real religious life?

LIBERTY AS SACRIFICE

We have one more question,
then, to ask ourselves. Having spoken briefly
about the liberty of choice and the liberty of
love, we ask: are there different levels or, from
another viewpoint, different degrees to loving?
Yes, there are. The highest is to sacrifice.

What does it mean to sacrifice? To sacrifice means to surrender something precious
for someone whom we love. It must be something precious. If we give away what is not
precious, that may be good business or good
riddance, but it is not sacrifice. And it must be
surrender. We must let go, give up. And let us
remember, we let go with our hearts; it's not
enough to let go with our hands.

Sacrifice, then, means surrender of something precious for the one whom we love. As
just described, sacrifice is the language of love.
It is the proof of love. It is the food of love. It
is the atmosphere of love. It is especially the
source of our growth in love. We let go of what
we like, and thus, this is precious to God, this

is sacrifice. But notice, not only must it be something precious—otherwise, we're not even making a sacrifice—but we must be deeply in love. And as every wife knows, in spite of all the romanticism of her husband, we sacrifice only to the degree to which we are in love. We are only as willing to surrender as we are in love with the one for whom we make the sacrifice.

We have one more question to ask. If sacrifice is the highest level of love, within sacrifice itself is there some highest and deepest surrender we can make? What is the most precious thing we have which we are most reluctant to surrender...? The most difficult surrender we all have to make is the surrender of self. Hence, that casual expression, *self-sacrifice*, is at the heart of Christian sanctity. "Self" is not just a casual prefix: it says everything.

It is sacrifice *by* the self. We freely make the sacrifice. Indeed, unless we do so freely, it's not even a sacrifice. Sacrifice can only be motivated by love. And we've already said that we love only when we want to. So self-sacrifice means that we choose to make the surrender.

A large part of our spiritual formation, which should go on through life, is to motivate ourselves to want to make the surrender. We don't do so simply because others are doing it, or because "it's something I've read about and it's a good thing," or because "I'm going to get something out of it." We motivate ourselves to want to sacrifice because we love the one for whom alone we make it.

Self-sacrifice is not only *by* the self, but also, what is so important, *of* the self. It is we who make the sacrifice; hence, the priestly function of our religious life — for a priest is one who offers sacrifice. But our sacrifice is also *of* the self, and that is the victim side of our religious life. It is we who make the surrender, and it is ourselves whom we surrender.

Needless to say, this is a lifetime task. After years in the religious life, we may think, "Well, I suppose this is it." Then we discover that there are whole areas of ourselves which we have not yet surrendered completely to God.

Sometimes God's demands seem very heavy. He is a jealous and demanding lover. Sometimes we may want to tell Him, "Lord, aren't You satisfied?" And He will say, "Not yet."

But here's the beauty of it. We know that God is grateful (strange words to use about God). We give ourselves to Him, and He gives Himself to us. To experience this response of God's love for us in return for our self-surrender to Him is worth all the sacrifice we make.

Even in this life, as I like to repeat, we should have a foretaste of heaven. We'd better! Otherwise, unless we knew where we were going, who would even want to go there? God wants us to be happy, not just in the distant, eschatological future, but here.

And He always comes through. He gives a joy that only He can give to those who surrender themselves to Him.

Religious Vocation— of Divine Origin

It is no secret to anyone familiar with the scene in countries like America, that two very different concepts of the religious life are widely professed.

One view sees religious life firmly rooted in history, tracing its lineage back through the founders of existing communities, through the great figures of Christian sanctity like Benedict, Dominic, Francis and Ignatius, like Angela Merici, Vincent de Paul and Frances de Chantal. It claims to have continuity with the unbroken tradition of Catholic Christianity, even to the early followers of the apostles who took literally Christ's invitation to follow Him the "whole way" in the practice of poverty, celibacy and obedience.

Clearly, in this view, religious life, while accommodating to each successive

age, has a definable past. And its present existence, so it is believed, has a confident future
because it is built on the foundation of—by now
—nineteen centuries of Christian experience.
It is, therefore, supported by the same Spirit
of Christ which has preserved the Church of
Christ, ever renewed yet always the same, in
spite of the ravages of time that have destroyed
empires and have seen even the greatest merely
human institutions decay.

Another view of religious life is not only
different but antithetical. It is willing to admit
the past, even to call it "a glorious past." But
it goes on to say that, in our age, this past is
gone; and all the wishful thinking or wistful
longing for its preservation has become fancy.

The religious life, as these proponents
see it, really has no past as a paradigm or pattern
of the present, but only a precarious and prob-
lematic future. What that future will be is
unclear and uncertain. It is part of that continu-
ing revelation which the Spirit of God is only
dimly showing now, and will perhaps gradually
disclose as the modern world slowly pene-
trates through the haze of conflicting ideologies
that envelop the western world like a dark cloud.

Needless to say, on its own premises,
this concept may still use the same term "religious life," and retain much of the vocabulary
which the historical view of religious life also
uses—but the meaning of words has been
radically changed.

Consequently the meaning of
religious vocation changes drastically, too. If

every vocation is somehow a personal response to an inner call, the response to becoming a religious is determined by one's notion of what a religious is supposed to be. On a lower key, for example, my intelligent response to wanting to become a medical doctor depends, finally, on some understanding of what the medical profession is all about. This, by the way, is a standard question asked by medical schools of all their applicants. In screening their overflow candidates, the last thing they want is a person who is vague and ambiguous about the profession he is aspiring to enter.

It would be useful to take each of these opposing views of religious life, and vocation, separately. And the analysis would be revealing. It would disclose that behind each view is really a different concept of the Church, in other words, a divergent ecclesiology. It would also show what many still are not convinced is true, that we are confronted here with more than semantics, more even than the familiar, and by now, pejorative adjectives "conservative" and "liberal," or worse still, "static" and "dynamic," might suggest.

My purpose is more specific. It is to state without apology that there is only one authentic concept of religious life, namely the first one; that its origins are divine because Christ, who is God, practiced this form of life, and to this day calls men and women to follow Him in living the way He did—a life of the evangelical counsels.

So we return to the subject of our conference: "Religious Vocation, of Divine Origin." My plan is to reflect on these facets of the subject: What does this mean? What are its theological implications? And what are some practical,

even critical, consequences in the promotion
of religious vocations?

THE MEANING

When we affirm that a reli-
gious vocation is of divine origin we exclude,
on principle, the claim that religious life—to
which vocations respond—is merely the product
of human genius.

Some would have us believe that religious
life came into the Church as a later (even late)
development of Christian civilization. We are
told various things: In the late third and early
fourth centuries certain Christians wished to
escape (with Pachomius) from the persecution
and immorality of the secular cities of Rome,
Alexandria and Antioch. So they fled to the
desert and formed communities where they
could live in protective custody from the temp-
tations and threats of a decadent paganism. We
are further assured that Benedict did much the
same thing in fleeing from the reality of a
barbarian invasion in his time. So, too, Francis
was a mystic who reacted against the dechris-
tianized luxury of his age. In the sixteenth
century, the Church needed a military leader
to defend the Papacy against the incursions of
Protestantism. Soon after, the Counter Reformation called for the establishment of Catholic schools. With the settlement of North and
South America, and more recently the coloniza-
tion of Asia and Africa—workers were needed in
orphanages and homes for the aged, in institutions of learning and care for the handicapped.

In each case, so the argument runs, a charis-
matic leader founded an organization to meet

the call of the times. No doubt inspired by Christian charity, members would be recruited to fulfill the obvious human needs and, presto, another religious community came into being.

Only that and nothing more? Yes, only that and nothing more.

Let me not be misunderstood. I am not denying that in too many cases, for which we are now paying a heavy price, vocations were recruited as the government might recruit men for the armed forces: to meet a certain quota of teachers, or nurses, or welfare workers, or administrators of institutions.

But an abuse of something is not the norm for understanding its meaning. When Canon Law was codified in 1917, and the Code made all sorts of detailed provisions for religious life — to prevent or at least reduce just such mistakes — that, too, was not normative of the essence of a religious vocation.

Its essence is to be found in the Gospels and therefore its origin must be traced, as the conciliar *Constitution on the Church* firmly declares, to "the teaching and example of the Lord."

Jesus Christ was the first religious. His life and preaching inspired men and women from the dawn of Christianity to sell all they had, give the proceeds to the poor and follow Him; to sacrifice, as He did, the legitimate rights to marriage and the rearing of a family; to be obedient, in a communitarian situation, to persons in whose directives they recognize the voice of God.

No one is saying that by the year 100 there were full-blown religious societies comparable to the highly structured and constitutional communities of today. But by the same token, no single mystery of the faith had the fullness of expression or clarity of comprehension it possesses now. There is such a thing as development of doctrine. The Real Presence or the Papal primacy, the life of grace or collegiality enjoy a depth of penetration and a degree of relevance that were simply not there in the year 100, or 700, or even 1900 A.D.

Saying that, however, is not to question—indeed, it positively affirms—that the substance and essentials of these cardinal mysteries of Christianity were already and certainly revealed by Christ and therefore present in the Church's bosom since the apostolic age.

THEOLOGICAL IMPLICATIONS

Once we admit that the quintessence of religious life is part of Christian revelation, a myriad of theological implications follows, out of which I will select only three: implications in Christology, in ecclesiology, and in ascetical theology.

Among the fundamental questions that Christologists have been asking is the one summarized in St. Anselm's famous work, *Cur Deus Homo?* "Why did God become man?"

The immediate and very correct answer is that God became man in order to save mankind, to redeem it from sin and rescue fallen man from the powers of darkness.

But if we keep pressing, and ask further: Was that all? we must say that God became man not only to save the world, but also to sanctify it; not only to deliver us sinners from sin, but also to lead us to holiness in union with Himself.

Correspondingly, then, we must say that Christ founded the Church not only as the great sacrament of salvation, but also as the sacrament of sanctification. In other words, He wants His faithful not only to be liberated from evil, but also to be raised to perfection. And He specially provided, within the Church, for religious to witness to holiness in their own lives so that, seeing their example and following their exhortation, others might be helped to reach holiness in the practice of virtue.

St. Paul's crisp mandate, "Be imitators of me, as I am of Christ," is a brief but telling summary of the main purpose of religious life, and so the principal motive that should attract religious vocations.

Moreover, the vocation is to no ordinary holiness, but to complete self-giving by a totality of duration, lifetime commitment; a totality of sacrifice, comprised in the three vows; and a totality of service, uniquely devoted to the sacralization of the world.

If we confused this invitation to holiness with the universal call to Christians to become Christlike, we would forget the lesson of God's selective call — since Abraham's time — to certain persons to be divinely chosen instruments of grace to their fellow men. To deny such providential selectivity is to become a victim of revolutionary egalitarianism which seeks to reduce the marvelous variety and social interdependence of human beings in God's world to the classless Utopia of a Marxist mythology.

Everything else is secondary and, as we are now sadly discovering, worse than useless in the absence of this primary focus. A religious may have other employments and engage in a variety of what we call apostolates. But his (or her) vocation is to holiness.

From an ecclesiological point of view, the divine origin of religious life implies that the preservation and interpretation, in fact the approbation and regulation of this life belong by divine right to the hierarchical Church, and ultimately to the Holy See.

This is no trivial observation. If, as Vatican II explicitly teaches, "the counsels are a divine gift, which the Church received from her Lord, and which she always safeguards with the help of His grace," then the guarantee of this grace in fostering and keeping religious vocations is conditioned on the humble acceptance in this matter of the Church's authoritative guidance.

Never has obedience to the Church's directives been more obviously and, by now, even pragmatically important. Nothing less than the survival of religious institutes is at stake.

As more than one commentator has pointed out, what major superiors in religious communities are being called on to do may be compared to the grave responsibility incumbent on bishops in the Catholic Church. Superiors, like bishops, are being tested, especially in their collegial loyalty to Rome, which means their collective conformity—what a painful word!—to the principles of the Church's historic teaching spelled out by the Second Vatican Council and mandated by the organs which the Vicar of Christ uses to direct the Church's policy.

It is at this point that a word must be said about legitimate pluralism among religious institutes. Their plurality is a matter of record, and their diversity is part of that breath-taking respect for tastes and temperaments so characteristic of God, in matters spiritual as in the natural and even political order. The United States is not Ceylon or Tanzania, and no two religious communities approved by the Church are, or are meant to be, quite the same. Some are more active, as we say, and others more contemplative; some are teaching children in grammar schools, and others are in charge of hospitals or homes for the aged; some are more loosely structured and draw one type of individual; others are more highly organized and appeal to another kind of personality; some are strictly monastic or approximate a monastic form, whereas others are more eremitic, with stress on the individual's role in the modern deserts of urban society.

Such variety is neither new nor unusual, and is meant to witness on earth to something of the infinitude of the heavenly Trinity.

Yet, just because this valid diversity is so precious, it needs the steady hand of the Church's divinely-promised assistance to keep it from turning into an indiscriminate mixture.

In the same way, within communities no two people are exactly alike, and the very definition of person as a distinct, autonomous individual suggests that no community could demand, even if it wanted to, absolute and regimented uniformity. Nor did we have to wait for recent psychologists to inform us about that.

Yet, again, just because this valid individuality is so precious, it needs the steady hand of the Church's guidance to preserve it from degenerating into egocentricity.

One of the ironies of our day is that Rome, which we refer to as the Church's center of unity, has become, for more than one country, protector of diversity among religious families and, inside communities, the defender of personal individuality. One reason is that a wave of conformism is in the air and, not infrequently, those in local authority (or at least in power) are trying to shape religious life to the homogeneous mass of some preconceived ideology.

What does the divine origin of religious life imply in the field of ascetical theology? Its most serious implication is that a religious vocation is to a state of life, that the words "state" and "stay" and "stable" are not merely common derivatives from the Latin verb *stare*, which means "to stand." They indicate what was taken for granted but in recent years is being challenged: that to those whom Christ calls to a religious institute He also gives the grace to remain faithful in their vocation all the days of their life.

We all know what happened: so many departures from the convent and religious life as have no parallel in modern history. Nothing like it had occurred, at least since the sixteenth century, and maybe never before in Catholic Christianity.

The resulting image in the minds of millions of people has been devastating. Instead of stability, instability; and instead of permanence, the impression left on the faithful is that vows are at best hopeful promises and at worst ephemeral gestures of fickle piety.

The issue is too complex to be examined in detail. One contributing factor, however, to this spirit of impermanence has been the false notion that religious life is actually a misnomer; that it is more like a religious mood. Once the mood passes, you leave, much as a person might change a job or place of residence, and often with less concern for the damaging consequences of his action.

All of this is a logical corollary to considering religious life only a human creation, subject to the same vicissitudes as every other human enterprise.

Today's world, it is argued, is characterized by a dizzy spell of change. Even the newly-coined expression "life-style" is symptomatic of the general trend. Styles change with the season, or the latest decision of the hidden persuaders in commercial advertising. So, too, one's life is expected to take on the same instability, and anyone who dares buck the trend is put down as "not with it" or "reactionary."

Hence the importance of recovering what ascetical writers had been saying all along, but complacently assumed that everyone believed. No matter how hectic the pace of modern times, and in spite of all the talk about "The Future Shock" induced by our unstable age, God's revealed truths remain essentially unchanged.

Among these truths is the fact that some people are divinely called to walk in the footsteps of the Master and duplicate His life of evangelical generosity.

Those who are thus called have His promise of staying in the state of life to which He invited them. Indeed, their stability is part of the very witness they are supposed to give of God's unchangeable presence in the midst of a fleeting world.

What is a Religious Community Today?

It may seem prosaic to ask such an obvious question: what is a religious community? But it is not prosaic to add the word "today," because if there was any doubt about the confusion in religious life a few years ago, it is perfectly plain now. And there is confusion in the religious life because there is uncertainty in many people's minds about it — not only about its refinements or subtleties, but also about its very essence.

The Second Vatican Council did not speak in vain when it spelled out, as had never been done in the history of the Church's ecumenical councils, the meaning of religious life, its essential qualities, and responsibilities.

157

Now you will want to look at yourselves more closely than ever before. In a word, you will want to establish your identity, to ask yourselves: who are we? what makes us what we are? Those institutes which finally face the question and honestly try to answer it will not only survive but in the years to come will flourish and do great things for God. The rest—and here I have some fifteen centuries of the Church's history to back me up on this statement—the rest I leave to the mercy of God's permissive providence. Humanly speaking—or better, historically speaking—their future is at best uncertain and at worst impossible.

My plan is to cover the matter in two parts of uneven length. In the first part I propose to analyze: what is a religious community? And to analyze it on two levels, the historical and the existential. Then more briefly, I wish to suggest some procedures for the immediate future. Let me begin by defining a religious community and go on to explain what I mean.

A religious community is a group of men or women with a common spiritual ancestry and secondly, a corporate history in living the evangelical counsels under the aegis of the Church. This I would call the historical dimension of a religious community. But, as we know, a community is also in existence. It has what I call an existential dimension. And here I would include four elements: a religious community is a community of faith, a community of worship, a community of labor, and a community of friendship.

HISTORICAL DIMENSION OF A RELIGIOUS COMMUNITY

We began by saying that a religious community has a common spiritual ancestry. Each congregation or religious order had a distinct founder or foundress, and sometimes, though rarely, more than one. This is not an episode or coincidence. It is of the essence of a religious society as a distinctive group of people in the Church. The founder or foundress is by God's will meant to be the foundation of the institute (and that is not merely a clever alliteration), on which foundation the society is to be built and apart from which its members are building on sand.

Each founder has his or her approach to God. And no single factor is more necessary for the members of a community than to identify this spirit, study its special understanding of the Gospel, and constantly seek to implement this vision in their lives. Thus the poverty of St. Francis should characterize Franciscans; the obedience of Ignatius should characterize the Jesuits; the contemplation of Teresa, the Carmelites; and so on for all religious families. Otherwise they are drifting on the shoals of chance and are in danger of becoming, as so many have in the past, useless in the Church of God. And they don't have to be put out of existence by imperial or royal mandates; historically they have dissolved themselves.

In the same way, each religious community has its own corporate history. From the time the rule or constitutions of an institute are approved by the Church, down through the years of its work in the apostolate, every community, like every person, has a biography. This biography is as much part of the community today as my personal experiences from infancy to the present moment are part of me. It is possible to forget or obscure this history or reduce it to a collection of interesting names, dates, and events neatly stacked up in the archives or published in a big, unreadable volume, but not without detriment to what a community is supposed to be.

Suppose I as a person were to suddenly lapse into amnesia and forget that I ever had a lifetime of joys and sorrows before me, or lost all my memory and could not recall whom I had known or what I had done or where I had been. Would I still call myself me in the same intelligible sense that I can if I do know who I am now because I know who I have been until now? Religious communities have a lot of homework to do in this regard, and the sooner they grasp this secret of self-identity by placing themselves in the context of their own history, the better for everyone in the community.

After all, the members of a community are not only the present statistical people who are on the roster; they are all the hundreds — and by now for some of you, thousands — who, faith tells us, are as alive as they ever were and in a true sense united in a community of spirit which transcends not only space but time. To know these members and to identify yourselves with them is to really know and, I would like to add, belong to your community. So much for the historical dimension.

EXISTENTIAL DIMENSION OF A RELIGIOUS COMMUNITY

But communities, as we know, are alive today. They are not only the large geographic bodies; they are also, and mainly, the local community—from two or three to two or three hundred and more, and usually a dozen or two who form the backbone of an international or national community. The distinction I want to make now is crucial because, after all, the statewide, national, or even international community is mainly a community of principle. I almost want to say it's a community on paper, whereas the smaller group is the real community. It is the community in practice. The first we talk about, think about, and write about; the second we live.

It is, therefore, the local community where the religious life is either lived well or poorly or—I am safe in saying in spite of claims to the contrary—is not being lived at all. And it is on this level that the communities of the future must stake their claims.

The religious community is first of all a community of faith. An authentic religious community is therefore a community of believers. I wish this could be taken for granted. But it's no platitude. Simple and strong acceptance of the cardinal mysteries of the Catholic

Faith is basic to a religious community and, sad to say, it cannot be presumed to be present nowadays. In other words, you cannot presume that every member of the community is a believing Catholic.

I would single out three mysteries of the faith as crucial: faith in Christ's divinity, in the Eucharist, and in the Roman primacy. These I consider the indispensable triad that either all the members of a community truly believe or that community is in grave difficulty. And a single unbeliever in a hundred is one too many.

Why these three truths of faith? Of the first two I will just make some passing comments; on the third I will spend a little more time.

Why the divinity of Christ as the first of what I consider the three cardinal mysteries of the faith that all members of a community must profess to insure its being a religious community? The reason is that it is Christ's divinity which gives substance to our life of the counsels because Jesus Christ was the first religious. He lived the religious life as a man, but we believe—believe, mind you —that this life is also worth living because we believe *that* Man is God.

Poverty, celibacy, and obedience—the essence of the counsels is intelligible and bearable only for those who are sustained through life by the conviction that He who is God lived this life, wants them to live it, and sustains them with His divine grace.

Why the Eucharist? Because the Eucharist as presence and liturgy is the only valid center of a religious community. Either Christ, reserved and worshiped in the Blessed Sacrament, is the Living Presence around whom the community is organized and that same Christ, worshiped daily in the liturgy, is the source of strength for that community, or that community's days are numbered. This was true way back in the early centuries of the Church; it is true now. A community is either Eucharistic or it ceases to be a religious institute.

The third, faith in the papal primacy. Why? Because I think that loyalty to the See of Peter is today as never before — even in the sixteenth century — the hallmark of a true Catholic. And no one can be a true religious unless he is also authentically Catholic.

Let me spell this out a bit more plainly. The issue at stake is: who has for us as religious the decisive authority to determine what the religious life ought to be? For as you know, the question is no longer: how do you live this life? The real question is: what is it?

In order to answer this basic question, I think we can line up the following set of principles, each following logically from the preceding:

1. The religious life is part of divine revelation, as stated by the Second Vatican Council in the sixth chapter of the Dogmatic Constitution on the Church. In substance, it says that the celibate life of poverty and obedience was first taught and practiced by Jesus Christ as found in the gospels. That statement should be carved in granite. It means, therefore, that our religious life is a mystery of faith revealed by God.

2. Since the religious state is a matter of revelation, only the Church founded by Christ has the divine right to preserve, interpret, and implement this form of life for the faithful. (Others might assume the right, but only the Church has it.)

3. Within the Church, only the Vicar of Christ, personally and through the agencies by which he guides the Church, has the final judgment on all matters affecting revelation — in this case, to safeguard, explain, and apply this part of the deposit of faith for the people.

4. Consequently, everyone else in the Church, including individual bishops or groups of bishops, must conform to the norms decisively approved by the Holy See, at the risk of being deprived of that guidance which the Holy Spirit gives to the Church, and here, to that part of the Church that wants to follow Christ in religious community.

So much for a religious community being a community of believers.

It is secondly a community of worship. By community of worship I mean regular prayer together, including the Eucharistic Liturgy. Why is this so important? Because of another cardinal principle of faith. Faith teaches us that in the order of revelation no individual can reach his destiny as an individual without grace. The ordinary way of obtaining grace is to ask for it. Those words of our Savior, "Ask and you shall receive," should be also restated, "If you do not ask, you shall not receive." But just as it is true for individuals, so is it true for societies where the essence of a society is to pursue a way of life that is supernatural. Unless that society as a corporate entity asks for grace, it cannot survive. And the obverse is what I have come to call "social Pelagianism."

In other words, to remain faithful to our convictions as religious, to continue doing as a group the apostolate to which Christ has called us, we need grace. In the ordinary providence of God, grace is given in answer to prayer — individual prayer for my salvation and sanctification, corporate prayer for corporate grace. In order to be able to live up to the high demands of poverty in an age and especially in a country of affluence, of chastity in an era gone mad with sex, and of obedience in a period of history in which the personal will of each human being, what he or she wants, is almost deified—to be able to live out this life corporately, we need corporate grace. To obtain it we must pray corporately. If we don't, the society does not receive the grace which it needs to survive.

Thirdly, *a religious community is a community of labor.* Religious communities are founded not for their own benefit alone, but for the good of the people of God. They were established as corporate apostolates. All religious communities began somehow as corporate apostolates in which like-minded, or better, like-hearted, persons banded together for a special work of mercy in the Church. Either communities today work together in what is sometimes pejoratively called "the institutional apostolate" or they will fall apart for the best of reasons—that is, because they no longer have a reason for existence.

This does not mean that each and every member is formally part of such a corporate enterprise. It does not mean that in every case, every day, or every hour of the day, each member is formally inside of the four walls of an institution which has the name of your community on the cornerstone or over the arch. But it does mean that the principal work of the community is a cooperative apostolate in schools, in hospitals, in groups, in all kinds of collaborative efforts.

(And by the way, I don't think I am being subtle in distinguishing between collaboration and cooperation. When you collaborate, you work together; the word cooperate, on the other hand, can cover a multitude of ways in which people who, from one end of the year to the next, never even sit down to a meal together, yet claim to be engaged in the cooperative enterprise. Collaboration means working together; I might say, sweating together.)

Corporate apostolate means that each considers the work of the community paramount, each is not jealous of what he or she is doing, but is happy to have others collaborate, and each is not envious of what someone else is doing, since the good of the whole is the good of each, and the success of the whole is considered the success of each.

So much for a religious community being a community of labor.

Finally, a religious community is *a community of friendship.* I thought for just a moment whether I shouldn't speak about "a community of love." I decided not to. There is more disharmony, disunity and sometimes even cynical hatred masking under the name of love than I think modern society has ever witnessed. So I speak of a community of friendship.

In talking about a community of friendship I will use the perpendicular pronoun because I feel safest in talking about that person called me: first, because it's my richest experience, and secondly, because nobody can question my having both the experience and the honesty to share this experience with you. A community of friendship is where I find my nearest and dearest friends. Now there will be others who will be very dear to me: my parents if they are still alive (though of course they are all very much alive), members of the family, people whom I have worked for. However, all other friendships in a true sense do not have what I would call the physiognomy of the friendships we should cultivate and experience in communities.

Thirdly, in a community of friendship I find the love which is the strongest desire of the human heart. In other words, I must find people who love me. I must discover among my fellow religious people who love me selflessly. In fact, I would distinguish love from friendship by saying that friendship is love in action. People talk about love; the poets write about it; only friends live it—when they love sincerely. In other words, friends who love me take me for what I am and show that their love is genuine, that they love me graciously, that they love me patiently— and this is the hardest. They accept me for what I am—a person, which by definition is an individual.

I trust you agree we all consider other people just a bit eccentric for the good reason that, humanly speaking, we all consider ourselves the center of our own little world. To give and take is to find the love that a community must have. If it doesn't, the human heart first begins to choke, then suffocates and the human spirit dies. The food of the spirit of man is love.

Moreover, the community of friendship is where I not only find love in others who love me, but where I find scope for the love that I want to give. Love is not only hungry, love is also generous. It is true love, therefore, when it seeks to give without looking for anything in return: for example, when I love those who are less lovable, though I may get only a frown or a cold stare in return. I call this practicing the apostolate of concern, by which I am concerned about my fellow religious—how they feel, what they are doing, what they are thinking, what they are planning. And, as I have told myself so often, one of the easiest ways of finding out is to ask them.

I therefore recognize from living in this kind of community that far from stultifying our capacity for love, our celibacy ennobles it and deepens it. Indeed, I don't hesitate to say that it makes it possible by giving us a heart which has been inspired by grace to find its greatest joy in giving joy to others.

So much for the existential dimension.

Now a recommendation and then an epilogue. I think we have come to a point in the religious life in the United States—not in all countries, by the way, but certainly in ours— where to just talk about the religious life, attend another conference, have another dialogue, is the last thing we need. This is the time for action. Let me suggest what needs to be done:

First, review your self-identity according to the mind of the Church.

Secondly, maintain religious community life — updated, of course, adjusted, of course, modern, of course — but in the true spirit of the Church and the teachings of the Apostolic See. Many girls have told me very frankly, "I would no more enter certain religious communities than I would marry an alcoholic — for the same reason: my life would be just as insecure." Your members and prospective members want to know that they are protected in their freedom to be religious according to the mind of the Church.

I began with an apology for talking about such a prosaic subject as: "What Is a Religious Community?" Now perhaps I should insist that what we have said is not poetic. The community that I described for you, besides being the kind of religious life which the Church in its highest authority has been telling us ought to be, is also the picture painted for us by St. Luke in the Acts of the Apostles, where he describes the religious community.

Since the time of that Jerusalem community, many have found what Christ wants us to find in a religious community on earth — the human counterpart to that community to which we are all aspiring, the City on High. Heaven is a community where faith becomes vision and where nothing but joy, happiness, and imperturbable peace reign, because all are united in Christ.

The Spiritual Personality of Religious Communities

Societies, like individuals, have distinct personalities. Or, more accurately, societies, no less than individuals, are as effective as they are distinctive, contributing their unique share to the welfare of mankind under the Providence of God.

Religious communities are no exception. They are so numerous in the Church, and so varied, because there are so many ways that Christ can be imitated — since God is infinite and Christ, who is divine, is infinitely imitable. They are also manifold because the Church wisely encourages different ways in which different groups can render varied service to the People of God — some by concentrating on prayerful contemplation and sacrifice, others by combining the roles of Mary and Martha through contemplation in action, and still others by moving rhythmically from prayer to action and back to prayer again.

They are further varied because the needs of the Church are so kaleidoscopic. In the Church are mothers who are giving birth to children, children of every age who need to be instructed; there are the sick and maimed, the weak and the handicapped; the confused who need counsel and the aged who wish to be cared for and loved.

And all the while we know that the corporal works of mercy are only the means for affecting spiritual change, even as Christ went about doing good to people's bodies in order to reach and transform their souls.

DISTINCTIVE IDENTITY

So much for the fact that there are different religious orders and congregations in the Church.

Our next question is: How do these differences arise or, from another viewpoint, how are they identified?

These differences arise in societies, no less than in individuals, mainly from two sources: from differences of origin and from each having a different history.

Suppose we look for a moment at each of ourselves. How come we are so different and therefore distinctive? Each of us had different parents, or if the same parents physically, parents who brought us into the world at different times, or even if by rare exception we were twins bodily, God infused different souls into these bodies at conception. In any case, our origins are unique. Each of us began as a distinct individual. Again, each of us, since conception and birth, has had his or her own history which we call our autobiography. Our experiences within and our experiences outside of us have been our own and no one else's.

As a consequence of both factors, of our unique origin and our own personal history, we are we. We are, in a word, distinct persons with distinct names that stand for distinct individuals. We have our own identity.

If we apply these two norms to the moral persons which are societies and, for our purpose, religious communities, we see the same principles operative.

Benedictines are not Franciscans, Dominicans are not Jesuits, Carthusians are not the Camaldolese, Ursulines are not the Sisters of Notre Dame, and so of all the religious families in the Church for two main reasons: because each religious family, and within the family each community, had its own founder or foundress who infused into it his or her distinctive spirit, and because this spirit, animating just this body of religious men or women, has had its own communitarian biography.

We could, at this point, begin to compare the relative importance of origins and history in distinguishing one religious community from another. But the comparison, though interesting, would not be very useful. Why not? Because in the life of societies as of individuals, the two elements are really inseparable.

Our origins will forever shape our history. And our history is the outgrowth and development (or regression) of our origins.

SPIRIT OF THE FOUNDERS

Yet between these two factors, there is no doubt which one is primary, not only in time because it came first but in essence because without it nothing else could follow.

It is the distinctive spirituality of the founders.

Taking stock of this priority, the Second Vatican Council declared: "It is for the good of the Church that institutes have their own proper characters and functions. Therefore the spirit and aims of each founder should be faithfully accepted and retained, as indeed should each institute's sound traditions, for all of these constitute the patrimony of the institute" *(Perfectae caritatis, 2).*

Thus, according to the mind of the Church the following principles of renewal (as the basis for adaptation to the times) are required:

1. Each religious institute should be distinctive. This is good for the Church, so that obscuring or blurring such distinctiveness is bad for the Church.

2. This distinctiveness consists in having a unique character (or personality) and what follows as a result, a special work in the apostolate. A characterless community is like a characterless individual. They are both ineffective. So, too, each community should concentrate on some particular apostolate — even though it may give attention to a variety of human needs. A scattered apostolic zeal going in all directions at once dissipates the energies of societies no less than it drains, with lowered achievement, the resources of persons.

3. Such community distinctiveness, the Church tells us, must first be acknowledged. A synonym for acknowledged is recognized, which means it must be identified. It is not something so vague and amorphous as to be unintelligible. Otherwise what good is it? And, once identified, it should at all costs be preserved.

4. Concretely the identity is recognized first in the spirit and intentions of the founders. Note that we have here two qualities of the founders which set the pattern for a religious institute.

— the spirit of the founder, which is his or her special charism or supernatural gift by which God animates this institute, and

— the aims or intentions of the founder, which are the purposes or goals he or she sought to be accomplished in and by this particular community: *in* the community through the special ways in which God would be honored and Christ the God-man would be imitated; and *by* the community through the special apostolic labors that its members would perform for the extension of God's Kingdom.

5. Also concretely the institute's identity is recognized in the sound traditions — let us stress *sound* traditions — which form its authentic heritage. These traditions are the founder's spirit lived out by those who inherited it.

6. Finally, and most pertinently, it does no good to merely recognize this identity. It must also, the Church reminds us, be preserved. Preservation of the community's identity is the indispensable precondition for valid renewal. Without it there is revolution but not renovation.

The Church wants religious institutes to
— *know* who they are, so that
— knowing who they are, they can then *be*
themselves.

Only on these conditions is it reasonable,
or even possible, to talk about adaptation to the
times or of adjustment to changing circumstances
of the age. Unless deep interior renewal, according to the spirit of the founder, precede adjustment to the times, the times will so completely
change an institute that it will even cease to
be a religious community. Adaptation becomes
senseless conformity whenever societies, no
less than individuals, forget their distinctive
personalities, when they barter their rights
to be themselves for the sake of temporary
expedience or the fear of a passing criticism of
not being relevant to the times.

O INTO THE FUTURE

One statement of the con-
ciliar decree on the up-to-date renewal of
religious life has been surprisingly overlooked
in much of the current writing on the subject.
It touches directly on our theme of "the one and
the many" in religious communities.

"Institutes and monasteries which the Holy
See, having consulted the local ordinaries concerned, judges not to offer any reasonable hope
of further development, are to be forbidden
to receive any more novices. If possible, they
are to be amalgamated with more flourishing
institutes or monasteries whose aims and spirit
differ little from their own" *(Perfectae caritatis,* 21).

Amalgamation with more flourishing institutes or monasteries is to be done, as far as possible, with communities that have more or less the same spirit. There is great wisdom in this recommendation. It presumes that where communities have either the same origin or the same original purpose in serving the Church, this kind of amalgamation is thoroughly feasible. So far from having to be mandated from above, it should be sought spontaneously (and realistically) by the handicapped communities themselves. Over the centuries it has often been accomplished with great benefit to everyone concerned.

But this also presumes that the amalgamation is done in favor of "more flourishing institutes or monasteries." By now it is becoming more and more clear which are the more flourishing communities. They are those that attract postulants and novices to their ranks because they offer a sound prospect of a lifetime commitment of sacrifice in the following of Christ and service of His Church.

Another recommendation of the Second Vatican Council deserves more attention than it has been getting. Having declared that amalgamations may be necessary to save some faltering communities, the council went on to favor the creation of federations, unions or associations with a view to strengthening their separate institutes.

"Institutes and monasteries should, as opportunity offers and with the approval of the Holy See, form federations, if they belong in some measure, to the same religious family. Failing this, they should form unions, if they have almost identical constitutions and customs, have the same spirit, and especially if they are few in number. Or they should form associations if they have the same or similar active apostolates" *(Perfectae caritatis, 22)*.

To be carefully noted is that three different terms are used to describe three very different kinds of cooperative enterprise, in varying degrees of coalition.

Common to all these ventures is that they be done with the approval of the Holy See. They also presume that, although juridically distinct, many communities either "belong to the same religious family," or "have almost identical constitutions and customs," or "have the same spirit," or at least "have the same or similar active apostolates." The implication is that today, perhaps more than ever before, there is need for collaboration. Individual communities, faced with the challenges of a communitarian age, are hard pressed to retain their identity and even their character as religious unless — paradoxically — they cooperate with like-minded communities to strengthen their own commitments as religious institutes in the Roman Catholic Church.

Where there is question of creating a formal union, the Church requires that there be kept in view "the particular character of each institute and the freedom of choice left to each individual religious" *(Ecclesiae sanctae, II, 40)*. Of more than passing importance, too, is the provision that "the good of the Church must be kept in view" *(Ibidem)*. This means many things, but it certainly includes the proviso that the basis of any union or federation be the teachings of the Church and not just the personal ideas of some individuals. After all what matters in things of the spirit is not the obvious strength that comes from created numbers but the invisible power of truth that comes from the uncreated God.

On the level of forming associations among communities that "have the same or similar active apostolates," this is a desideratum that not only the Church's wisdom but the complexity of the modern age recommends. But again a proviso. This presumes that the grounds of association are those of the Church's hierarchy, under the See of Peter, which is "guided by the Holy Spirit" to guide religious in their distinctive pursuit of holiness among the People of God.